Hunger on Planet Earth

HUNGER ON PLANET EARTH

JULES ARCHER

Illustrated with photographs

Thomas Y. Crowell Company

New York

By the Author

Washington vs. Main Street:
The Struggle Between Federal
and Local Power

Watergate: America in Crisis

Hunger on Planet Earth

Manufactured in the United States of America

Library of Congress Cataloging in Publication Data
Archer, Jules. Hunger on planet Earth.

Bibliography: p.   SUMMARY: Explores the problem of the world's lack of sufficient food to feed its ever-increasing population. 1. Food supply— Juv. lit. 2. Starvation—Juv. lit. [1. Food supply. 2. Starvation] I. Title.
HD9000.5.A72 1976   338.1′9   76-3603   ISBN 0-690-01126-1

10 9 8 7 6 5 4 3 2 1

*For all the hungry people
who share our planet
but not its food*

Acknowledgments

For their generous assistance, I am obligated to Norman R. Michie, information liaison officer of the Food and Agriculture Organization of the United Nations; to Maryellen Hausman, communications director of the United States Committee for UNICEF; to Carol Terry, associate Quaker representative for the Quaker Office at the United Nations; to Joan Bush, information liaison officer of the World Health Organization of the United Nations; to Betty Hooper, information specialist, U.S. Center for Disease Control; and to Mary Lou Alm of the Pine Plains Library and Christine Crouch of the Mid-Hudson Library System.

I am also indebted to U.S. senator Ernest F. Hollings of South Carolina for permission to quote excerpts from his book, The Case Against Hunger.

J.A.

Pine Plains, New York

Contents

1

Will This Be Our World in 1997?

One day, not too far in the future, Americans may turn on their "wallvision" sets and hear a shocking speech from their president:

"Mr. Speaker, members of Congress, fellow Americans. It is with heavy heart that I deliver this State of the Union message tonight. Unlike some government leaders who fear panic if their people learn the full truth, I will not attempt to minimize the seriousness of the catastrophe that has befallen our planet. I am confident that Americans would want me to tell them honestly what sacrifices are necessary for our survival.

"The basic problem, of course, is that almost 7 billion men, women, and children are now struggling to survive on a planet that cannot adequately feed 3 billion people.

"The United States is one of the fortunate few nations of the world not faced by the immediate threat of mass starvation. But the new crisis precipitated by prolonged droughts in many parts of the earth must ultimately threaten us, too.

"These droughts have spread across the world in great hot, dusty waves. Famine stalks many lands where people and rats fight over the few blackened stalks thrusting through the cracked earth. There are even rumors of cannibalism in some countries. In Peru whole villages of dead people lie unburied because there are no survivors to bury them. In India funeral teams are working around the clock to collect and pile corpses in huge mounds for cremation, to prevent pestilence.

"Already 60 million people are known to have perished of starvation. An estimated billion are bare skin and bones. The bonds of family and society are breaking down in country after country. It is every man for himself as people search for enough food to stay alive, often abandoning their children to die. In Guatemala all the trees are stripped of bark— the final meals of families awaiting death.

"The crisis is producing great political turmoil which threatens the peace of the world. Upheavals are occurring, not in those countries with mass starvation where the people are too feeble and apathetic to revolt, but in countries where there is just enough food to keep people hungry and desperate.

"Last week alone we saw four revolutions break out. Two of the new governments are now threatening to go to war to seize food. One leader who has urged his nation to attack its neighbor argues that even if they lose, the casualties that they suffer will greatly reduce the number of people they have to feed.

"The hunger crisis has also loosed dreadful epidemics upon the world. Starving people cannot withstand disease. Typhus is raging in Turkey and Afghanistan. Cholera and plague are killing hundreds of thousands in Laos and Cambodia. Relapsing fever and tuberculosis are sweeping Africa. Travelers returning to London from Lebanon have brought back a virulent new flu for which there is no vaccine, and cases have already turned up in New York and Ohio.

"There are riots everywhere. All through the Middle East desperate mobs are attacking warehouses in search of food. Instead of stopping them, hungry soldiers and police are joining them. Last week when hundreds of thousands of rioters stormed the palace of one shah, demanding food, the shah's air force drove them off by spraying poison gas, killing more than 10,000 people.

"Food shortages in Europe and the Near East have sent crime rates soaring. Desperate people are committing crimes in broad daylight, on the busiest streets, to keep themselves and their families from starving. An all-pervading fear is spreading through Europe, where steep increases in heart disease, ulcers, mental breakdowns, and suicides are reported.

"People everywhere are losing hope in the future. Some Americans try to shut out the world's suffering by refusing to watch scenes of famine and food riots on wallvision news. But can we really sleep peacefully at night, unhaunted by dreams of starving children pleading with us not to let them die?

"We must recognize that if we do not help to force back the rising tide of hunger on earth, it will eventually engulf us as well. Drought respects no national boundaries. Changing weather patterns in the world today represent as serious a threat to the United States as to other nations.

"For a long time meteorologists have been warning us that dramatic changes were occurring in the earth's weather patterns, affecting food production. The climate has been steadily cooling down in the northern regions, bringing long freezes. The wheat-growing season in Canada and the Soviet Union has been shortened, and crops in northern Europe have been curtailed.

"At the same time the temperature has risen in the

equatorial belt, causing droughts and extended dry spells, followed by disastrous flooding. We can no longer count on the mild, balanced weather we enjoyed for most of this century.

"We need to understand that even the smallest changes in average temperature can play havoc with the world's food supply. During the great ice ages the earth's average temperature was only seven degrees lower than normal. We have now slid about one-fifth of the way back toward the average temperature of the ice ages. Each year deepens the chilling process a little more.

"Meanwhile, in North Central Africa the sands of the Sahara have continued speeding southward at a pace of more than thirty miles a year, destroying more and more food-growing lands.

"The world's scientists have told us that we Americans are partly responsible for these unfortunate weather changes. The particles of industrial pollution that we put into the air deflect sunlight back into space before it can reach and warm the earth's surface, thus cooling the northern regions. American farmers are concerned about a sharp decrease in the amount of sunshine reaching their crops.

"In the last decade our industrial expansion has increased contaminants in our atmosphere by more than 1,000 per cent. Our weather changes, of course, affect other continents as well. A shift in the earth's jet stream is now turning many of the world's farming regions into barren deserts.

"Food shortages are only part of the story. The grim fact is that our planet is now badly overcrowded. In the last quarter of a century alone, the world's population has increased by 93 per cent. There are now almost twice as many mouths to feed as there were in 1972. In the hungriest nations the population jump has been an appalling 160 per cent.

"To make room for the 25 million additional Americans born during the last two decades, we have built new megalopolises of concrete and glass that stretch for endless miles. They stand on huge areas of former farmland which might otherwise now be helping to feed a hungry world.

"We have paid other prices as well. Bumper-to-bumper traffic has become a way of life on our highways, with traffic jams lasting six and seven hours. Each week up to two dozen riders on subways are crushed or suffocated to death. Our schoolrooms are bursting, with chairs in every aisle. Hospitals and other services are almost paralyzed. For millions water is either rationed or prohibitively expensive. In polluted New York, Pittsburgh, and Los Angeles, people are compelled to go to work in face masks.

"My administration has been criticized for distributing free supplies of the tranquilizer H-231 to citizens forced to live in the cities of America. It is estimated that more than 176 million people now take H-231 daily. But if the government had *not* taken this step to protect public tranquility, we would now be experiencing an appalling jump in crimes of violence resulting from the frustrations of living under conditions of intolerable overcrowding.

"It is clear that we can no longer afford the luxury of individual choice about having children, and how many. That is why three weeks ago I sent Congress a bill requiring sterilization of mothers after the birth of a first child. I fully recognize that this bill is highly controversial. But what other option have we? Unless we shrink our population, our dwindling supplies of food and space will soon be exhausted.

"We are also preparing a bill to prohibit the sale of any more agricultural land for nonfarm purposes. It is shocking to realize that California, once a great region of fruit and vegetable farms, has now lost 77 per cent of its prime cropland to industry, shopping centers, and housing.

"We must face the fact that we have barely food enough at the present time to feed our own people adequately, let alone help the starving billions of the world. Our reserves of corn, rye, beans, peas, soybeans, and sugar have vanished. Our farmers are also suffering from crippling shortages of vital materials such as fertilizer, gas, baling wire, and tractor parts at a time when we need capacity production.

"We shall have to be willing to experiment with new sources of nutrition unfamiliar in our diet. That is why in 1995 I initiated a $3 billion crash program of food research. Our scientists have already developed important new foods. The peels of oranges and bananas have been pressed into nutritive juices. Food pastes made of tree leaves offer nourishing concentrates. Excellent protein is available in spreads made of processed insects. To replace shortages of commercial fish, we must learn to eat squid, seasnake, and seaweed. Once we grow accustomed to these highly nutritious new foods, we may even come to regard them as delicacies.

"We face another grave danger. Our scientists warn that the overfishing and pollution of the seas is turning all oceans into enormous cesspools. Huge blooms of poisonous diatoms are killing off marine life beneath. Vast floats of dead fish have raised intolerable stenches off the coasts of Chile, Peru, and Mexico. Meteorologists say the ocean's growing film of decayed matter is interfering with evaporation, worsening the rainfall shortage responsible for droughts.

"They also warn that the extinction of plankton algae, added to the reduction of land vegetation, is reducing the supply of oxygen we breathe. If we allow the oceans to die, mankind, too, will perish.

"Some scientists predict that within a century decaying matter in the seas will block the heat that normally radiates outward from earth to space, causing sea-level temperatures to rise sharply. If this heat melts the icecaps at both Poles, the oceans could rise by 100 feet or more, flooding the world's coastal cities. A third of the earth's people would be driven inland, further mobbing congested land areas.

"For these reasons our government joined last year with forty countries of Europe, South America, and Asia in setting up an International Sea Patrol, which has the power to detect and stop any nation responsible for dumping chemical wastes, spilling oil, leaking pesticides into the sea, or making illegal mass kills of fish.

"The starving billions in the world today are fearful reminders that the hour is late. Let us not forget the biblical example of Joseph, who saved the Egyptians by storing food during seven years of prosperity, enabling them to survive the seven years of famine that followed. We must begin cutting back our food consumption to build up emergency reserves for the famine years we may face if the pattern of worsening weather conditions continues.

"I urge every American to begin eliminating one item of food at *every* meal, starting tomorrow. Not only will we be leaner and healthier for it, but we can then begin stockpiling the food saved. I am asking our UN delegation to submit a similar resolution for adoption by all of the developed nations. We will also propose compulsory sterilization after the first child for *all* countries. The world must face the fact that if we do not conserve food by practicing life control, we shall have to do so by death control.

"Just last month a South American statesman declared, 'We must reappraise our system of medicine, so that we do not seek to keep alive those suffering from chronic disease or malnutrition, for whom death would be more merciful. Food for the living is more imperative than food for the dying.'

"Food shortages have already driven some governments to desperate measures. I was shocked to learn, through our intelligence services, that at least one country is secretly contaminating a percentage of marketed food eaten by its poorest classes with a toxin that causes fatal illness. Official blame is put on a new strain of flu. About 15 per cent of the population has already been poisoned in this manner.

"My fellow Americans, this life raft of earth is all we have in the sea of the universe. We cannot let half of it sink, for we will drown, too. That is why we and all nations are rushing to cooperate for mutual survival as never before.

"In the International Climate Control Commission, we and seventy-one other governments are seeking ways of creating weather patterns favorable to food production. To provide an equal distribution of sunlight and rain over all latitudes between 30° south and 60° north, we are experimenting with large reflecting satellites that concentrate heat and disperse clouds over selected farming regions.

"European nations are building a huge double air pipe under the Mediterranean to blow compressed dry air north and cool damp air south.

"Soviet, American, and Canadian meteorologists are working on plans to dam the Bering Strait, then channel warm water north to melt the Arctic icecap. We hope that the rise in temperature will make it possible to turn huge areas of Alaska, Siberia, and northern Canada into fertile farmland.

"In cooperation with the Arab states, we are developing extensive irrigation projects in the arid regions of the world by desalting salt water. With France and Germany we are involved in Project Mediterranean, planning to build an experimental city on the ocean floor which will subsist entirely on sea agriculture.

"With the Soviet Union we are developing Project Space Colony, which hopes to establish the first space station complex capable of supporting 10,000 people by the year 2012. Not only will they grow their own food by solar radiation and hydroponics, but they will also beam solar energy back to earth through giant reflecting mirrors.

"Migration to the moon and nearby planets, as urged by the National Welfare Conference, is under careful study. Starting a moon colony in collaboration with the Soviet Union will be a feasible option once we can further reduce the present cost of rocket travel. An international committee of biologists has already solved the problems of supplying water, air, and food to lunar settlers. Applying intense heat to moon rocks will provide fresh water and oxygen.

"The lunar surface is covered with rock fragments that could also be transformed into productive soil by adding water, mineral nutrients, and organic fibers. Lunar horticulture would use small leafy plants, maturing in the two-week periods of uninterrupted sunlight under air-tight plastic covers. Their leafage would provide nutritious proteins.

"Such are our hopes for the twenty-first century we are about to enter. But, my fellow Americans, we cannot postpone taking immediate action to deal with the urgent crisis of world hunger which is now upon us. Over thirty years ago a group of thirty-eight distinguished Nobel Prize winners, led by Sir Julian Huxley, issued a warning which was not heeded then, but which we can ignore today only at great peril.

"'Unless a favorable balance of population and resources is achieved with a minimum of delay,' they predicted, 'there is in prospect a Dark Age of human misery, famine, undereducation, and unrest which could generate growing panic, exploding into wars fought to appropriate the dwindling means of survival.' We are now at the threshold of that Dark Age.

"It will take superhuman efforts by all of us to keep from plunging into it. I ask all Americans to join with me now in cheerfully accepting the necessity of eating smaller meals, buying unfamiliar foods, raising fewer children, and paying higher taxes so that we can help save a billion of the world's people from death by starvation.

"We must consider these the dues of membership in the human race. I know that I can count on each of you to make the sacrifices essential to the survival of all of us who ride the planet Earth together.

"Thank you and good night."

You have been listening to the State of the Union address delivered by the president. Underlining the president's message comes word tonight from our correspondent in Dallas that the twelve-foot electrified fence erected all along the U.S.-Mexican border in 1994 has been blown open at points in Texas, California, and New Mexico.

An estimated total of 100,000 hungry Mexicans are reported rushing through the gaps seeking food on the American side of the border. Clashes have been reported with National Guard units and police in San Diego, Las Cruces, El Paso, and Laredo. One unconfirmed report puts known dead at more than 400 so far. We will interrupt our regular programming with the latest bulletins on this new crisis.

2
Crisis Conference in Rome

That chilling glimpse into the future is at present only science fiction. But its prognostications of things to come before the end of the century are based on the predictions of serious scientists of our time. If we do not awaken to our danger now, the year 1997 may indeed bring famine, wars, revolutions, mass terror, and epidemics.

By 1974 we were already in a crisis precipitated by adverse weather conditions. Severe drought had struck southern Asia, East Africa, the Sahel region of Africa, the two Yemens, and parts of Latin America. Torrential flooding ruined crops in northern India, Pakistan, and Bangladesh. The breadbasket of the world, the United States and Canada, suffered sharp declines in corn, grain, and soybean harvests because of a rainy spring, followed by summer drought and early frost.

The United Nations estimated that 460 million people were going to bed hungry every night, half of them children. UN secretary-general Kurt Waldheim flew to Africa in 1974 to inspect conditions in six nations of the Sahel region—Mali, Mauritania, Senegal, Upper Volta, Niger, and Chad.

The 20 million inhabitants of the Sahel are among the

world's poorest people—cattle-raising nomads and subsistence farmers who barely manage to stay alive. Waldheim was shaken by what he saw in the lands bordering the Sahara Desert. Children with matchstick legs and swollen bellies and emaciated adults were dying not only of hunger but also of measles, influenza, and cholera. Millions of refugees were streaming southward into filthy, overcrowded camps where there was not enough food to feed them.

A Norwegian relief team came upon one small village completely deserted except for sixty-two unburied corpses, all famine victims. Danakil tribesmen were found dead with dirt-filled mouths. "Only the vultures are fat," noted *Time* correspondent Lee Griggs.

Some proud African heads of state sought to conceal the severity of the famine, considering it humiliating to acknowledge that they were helpless to cope with the crisis. In Ethiopia, when hordes of desperate men, women, and chil-

A Mauritanian nomad holds a leather waterbag while his son drinks. (FAO)

dren fled drought-stricken Wollo province to surge into Addis Ababa, city authorities swiftly rounded them up, put them in jail, and left them to starve. Fear of offending Emperor Haile Selassie led even UN officials of the Food and Agriculture Organization (FAO) to mute its own field reports of mass hunger in Ethiopia.

After more than 100,000 Ethiopians had starved to death, flooding rains finally fell. Many survivors drowned in just a few inches of water because they were too weak to lift their heads to save themselves.

The Sahel landscape was littered with millions of dead sheep, cattle, and goats, which had been mainstays of life for the region's nomadic herdsmen. One tribal chief, staring at the animal carcasses and withered grazing lands, said sadly, "I am witnessing the burial of my ancestral village."

As the drought dried Lake Chad to a muddy trough, the people of Chad and Senegal ate leaves and roots to stay alive. In Niger diseased animals were eaten as fast as they fell, with the animals' blood reserved for children. In Senegal famished herdsmen sought to sell their last few scrawny cattle for some grain before the beasts collapsed.

In the goatskin tents of Mali's packed refugee camps, mothers with no milk left in their breasts watched their babies die beside them. French army planes airdropped bags of grain in the desert. When some burst open, women fell to their knees to sift the sands, retrieving every precious kernel.

In the refugee camps of Niger, gaunt Tuareg tribesmen resigned themselves to death after their camels starved. "When the camel collapses," goes an old Tuareg saying, "the game is over." Some tribesmen struggled to survive by cooking camel dung.

In Asia the plight of hungry people was equally desperate. Weeping mothers in Bengal looked on helplessly as their emaciated babies died. One woman collapsed only a few steps before she could reach a food relief distribution van, her tongue moving in and out. A relief worker withheld gruel, explaining, "It would finish her off right away."

Having stripped the trees of all edible leaves, entire families in India committed suicide to escape the agony of slow death by starvation.

Disastrous floods destroyed the rice crop of Bangladesh, where 75 million people were crowded into an area the size of Arkansas (population 2 million). Despair and the stench of death were everywhere. Farmer Pabchanad Pramanik, wiped out by the flood, had a wife and seven daughters to support. He received a daily relief ration of only nine ounces of rice—half the minimum needed by *one* person for bare survival. "We are in the hands of God," Pabchanad said.

The world food crisis of 1974 was brought about by a combination of misfortunes. Adverse weather caused crop failure and shortages simultaneously in the USSR, China, India, Australia, the African Sahel, and Southeast Asia. Heavy bidding for the wheat surpluses of the exporting countries priced the poor countries out of the market. The United States, its grain reserves severely drained, felt compelled to cut back its food aid program for hungry countries.

But mass starvation is nothing new in world history.

Most recorded famines have resulted from widespread crop failures caused by droughts, followed by dust storms and loss of seeds; by crop diseases and pests like locusts; by the disruption of wars and civil disturbances; and by natural disasters such as floods and earthquakes.

The Scriptures tell us of famines in ancient Palestine. In the Roman famine of 436 B.C. thousands of starving people threw themselves into the Tiber to end their misery. In the Irish famine of A.D. 192 hunger was so great "that lands and houses, territories and tribes, were emptied." In A.D. 272 Britons were reduced to eating the bark of trees and roots, and a famine thirty-eight years later killed at least 40,000.

In the Italy of A.D. 450 starving parents ate their children, anticipating satirist Jonathan Swift's bitter *Modest Proposal* (1729), in which he suggested that children in hungry Ireland be fattened and sold to the rich as food. During an Irish famine in A.D. 963, desperate parents went as far as trading their children for food.

In 1123 English starvation "let lifeless bodies lie unburied everywhere in cities, villages, and crossroads." A 1347 famine in Italy killed off two-thirds of the population.

A great famine in India occurred in 1769. Ten million people starved to death, leaving the air "so infected by the noxious effluvia of dead bodies" and rent by cries of the dying that few dared venture on the streets.

During Ireland's six-year potato famine, beginning in 1847, more than one million people died either of starvation or the pestilence that followed it. Another million fled to America, a fourth of them perishing within a year of departure.

More than 10 million lives were lost in the terrible famine

"Parents selling their children" in the terrible famine of 1877, as depicted by a Chinese artist of that time. (NEW YORK PUBLIC LIBRARY PICTURE COLLECTION)

that swept over China in 1877. "The people's faces are black with hunger; they are dying by thousands upon thousands," reported a Western traveler. "Women and girls and boys are openly offered for sale to any chance wayfarer. . . . A respectable married woman could be easily bought for six dollars, and a little girl for two. . . . Parents have been known to kill their children sooner than witness their prolonged sufferings, killing themselves afterward."

In 1889, as the British were making war in the Sudan, a plague of locusts swarmed over the fields beside the Nile. Carpeting roads and farms a foot deep, they stripped the grain bare. Many starving Egyptians turned to cannibalism. Others perished in the streets or on the banks of the Nile, whose waters were soon black with bodies.

In the early years of this century a first feeble effort to do something about world hunger led to the creation of an International Institute of Agriculture, with offices at Rome. Meagerly financed, it could only collect crop statistics and circulate information that it hoped would help to improve harvests.

In 1945 it was taken over by the newly formed United Nations, which transformed it into the World Food and Agriculture Organization. The FAO, observed the British journal *The Economist* sarcastically, was "a permanent institution devoted to proving there is not enough food in the world." Without real power, it could only prod the conscience of the world's wealthier nations into accepting responsibility for hunger in the poorer ("underdeveloped" or "developing") countries.

FAO director Lord Boyd Orr called a Famine Conference in Washington the following year. The twenty-three nations attending set up an International Emergency Food Council which, for three years after World War II, managed to avert famine by an equitable distribution of available surplus food.

Since 1950, however, famine has been caused by floods, droughts, and civil disorders in India, Pakistan, and Bangladesh; by locusts and earthquakes in the Middle East; by floods and agricultural mistakes in China; by earthquakes in Latin America; and by droughts and civil wars in Africa.

The delicate balance of the world's food supply was thrown badly out of whack in the early 1970's, when several years of crop failure were followed by an enormous price hike for oil by the Organization of Petroleum Exporting Countries (OPEC). The high cost of oil-based fertilizer forced the poorer nations to cut its use by a third. Already suffering from poor harvests caused by drought, they were now even worse off than before.

In December 1973 the FAO shocked the world by revealing that there was only enough reserve food grain on hand to feed the world for a month if it were needed. "We cannot get through the next six to twelve months without disaster," warned FAO official Charles Weitz. A group of Third World (neither pro-Soviet nor pro-American) nations meeting in Algiers called for an emergency World Food Conference, a call endorsed by U.S. secretary of state Henry Kissinger at the UN in September 1973.

On December 17 the UN decided to call a World Food Conference whose task would be "developing ways and means whereby the international community as a whole could take specific action to resolve the world food problem." The intention was to develop a long-range program.

But the immediate food situation deteriorated so rapidly that great pressure from the public and the delegates compelled the Conference to change its scope and give specific attention to the emergency when it opened on November 5, 1974, in the cavernous Palace of Congress at Rome.

For ten days some 1,250 world delegates, 300 representatives of private aid organizations, and 165 UN officials consulted on ways to solve the world's problem of hunger and malnutrition, both the immediate crisis and the long-term dilemma.

To symbolize the obligation of the world's haves to the

have-nots, a "scale of justice" was set up in the hall, with delegates invited to weigh themselves. They were then taxed on overweight, a tax allocated to feeding the hungry.

Addressing the opening session in front of a great blue backdrop emblazoned with the white UN emblem, Kissinger declared, "Today we must proclaim a bold objective, that within a decade no child will go to bed hungry, that no family will fear for its next day's bread, and that no human being's future and capacities will be stunted by malnutrition." But it soon became apparent that the wealthier nations, with inflation at home and food reserves at a low ebb, were seeking to substitute rhetoric for action to meet the immediate emergency.

Dr. Norman Borlaug, Nobel Prize winner for his contributions to agricultural science, angrily proposed locking up Kissinger and a dozen other leading delegates in a room without food for ten days, until they agreed to prompt measures to aid the thirty-two nations which were desperately short of food.

When the delegates' restaurant served lasagna, cutlet Milanese style, peas in butter, fruit, and wine, Canadian political scientist David Runnalls protested that a Spartan box lunch should have been served instead. "We're talking about a million people starving to death!" he pointed out.

Kissinger sought to discourage expectations that the United States, which had provided 84 per cent of all food aid contributed between 1965 and 1972, could continue to carry the burden of world famine relief. He pointed out that if the population of the poorer nations continued to increase by 2 per cent a year, their food needs would rise from 25 to 85 million tons by 1985.

"The world has come to depend on a few exporting countries, and particularly the United States, to maintain the necessary reserves," he said. "But reserves no longer exist, despite the fact that the United States has removed virtually all of its restrictions on production and our farmers have made an all-out effort to maximize output."

Kissinger's resistance to Conference pressures reflected the irritation of the American public, which had seen its grocery bills soar 36 per cent in two years because of shortages caused by a sharp rise in food exports, at being asked to permit even more food to leave the country as aid to the hungry nations.

Kissinger suggested that the world should look to the countries of the OPEC oil cartel for more aid, since they had intensified the food crisis by jumping oil prices 400 per cent in a single year. Their profiteering had robbed the poorer nations of badly needed fertilizer. "The oil exporters have a special responsibility in this regard," Kissinger insisted. "Ways must be found to move more of the surplus oil revenues into long-term lending or grants to poorer countries."

Niger's president, Hamani Diori, was critical of the minimal aid offered by the United States and other wealthy nations to the suffering Sahel. "The poorer you are," he complained, "the less you get."

UN secretary-general Waldheim called the disparity between the way rich and poor nations eat "indefensible in periods of shortage." Agreeing, Senator Hubert Humphrey urged each American to eat just one less hamburger a week, so that some 10 million additional tons of grain a year could be released to the hungry nations.

Scoffing at this suggestion as "clearly nonsense," Earl Butz, U.S. secretary of agriculture, blamed world food shortages on governments that failed to give farmers sufficient capitalist incentive for producing more. He refused to make a public pledge of additional American aid.

The Conference acknowledged that poor countries would have to increase their own food production and reduce their dependence on imports. But it was recognized that they

Secretary of Agriculture Earl Butz was criticized both at home and abroad for his reluctance to pledge U.S. aid. (GAMBLE/ NASHVILLE BANNER)

would still need imported grain for at least another ten to fifteen years. The Conference therefore called for a reduction in meat eating by the wealthier countries, so that more lands now growing feed for livestock could be planted instead to cereals for humans.

A global information and early warning system was set up to spot countries and regions threatened by food shortages and malnutrition, and to monitor the world food supply in order to rush aid where it was most urgently needed. This would be done through a world food security system that could call upon reserves held in the developed countries.

Left unresolved was how to meet the immediate crisis. The United States refused to make any commitment of additional grain aid from its commercial stocks. When Canada agreed to increase its aid by 20 per cent over the next three years, Senators George McGovern, Hubert Humphrey, and Dick Clark bitterly denounced the Ford administration's position as miserly and callous. Under fire, Secretary Butz finally felt compelled to agree to more U.S. assistance to the hungry nations.

The World Food Conference was disappointing because it had failed to compel the wealthy nations to cooperate in confronting the hunger crisis swiftly and unequivocally. It was estimated that in Bangladesh alone, a million people would die of starvation within six weeks after the Conference.

Rev. Arthur McCormack, a British priest active in aid to poor countries, said, "If beautiful speeches could cure hunger, we've got it made." On the other hand, Ludongo Mumeka, the Zambian delegate, defended the accomplishments of the Conference as a valuable first step. The poorer nations, he said, had not expected the delegates to be able to grow the food for them overnight in Rome.

Aided by cargos from many nations, the FAO managed to airlift food into crisis areas. But the amount represented only a bare fraction of the need. In Mali, which desperately required 300,000 tons of food, only 1,500 tons a month were flown in. Thousands of miles of desert, crumbling roads, and the lack of trucks added to the problem of getting what little food there was to the starving people.

Canon Burgess Carr, general secretary of the All Africa Conference of Churches, protested the reluctant response of the West to the African plight. The reason, he charged, was that the affected countries are neither politically nor economically significant. "To the West it's just 10 million niggers dying," he said angrily.

There are 2 billion people in the underdeveloped nations of the world. "One-third to one-half . . . suffer from hunger and malnutrition," pointed out Robert S. McNamara, president of the World Bank, "and 20 to 25 per cent of their children die before their fifth birthdays."

It is likely to become increasingly difficult for the relatively affluent one-third of mankind to ignore the cries of hunger from two-thirds of the world.

"There will be suffering and desperation on a scale as yet unknown," warned British scientist C. P. Snow. "This suffering will be witnessed—since our communications will be even better—by the advanced countries. . . . It is hard to imagine the psychological and political conditions which will be created by such a gap. . . . The rich populations will feel they are in a state of siege."

Four months after the crisis conference in Rome, Earl Butz finally announced in March 1975 that the Ford administration would commit more than 5.5 million tons of food aid to the world's hungry that year, an increase of $600 million in aid over 1974. But Fred Devine, deputy director of CARE, pointed out that because of American procrastination, "a lot of people will die, and others will become mentally retarded and physically deformed." The Catholic Relief Services also blamed the government for not having acted swiftly enough to head off disaster.

If the United States remains seriously committed to alleviating world hunger in the years ahead, many economists predict that Americans will have to accept one meatless and one breadless day a week. Cargill, Inc., a major grain exporter, reported that reduced supplies would no longer support American food consumption at the levels of 1974 and 1975. "Rationing must occur in both domestic and export consumption," the company warned.

In January 1975, President Ford applied controls that allowed him to monitor the size and destination of grain shipments. The new regulations would presumably assure poor nations that available American surpluses would be shared fairly, even if an equitable division led to food rationing here.

But can even the most sincere American efforts prevent hunger in a world where each year the human race grows by 2 per cent while eating 3.1 per cent more grain?

3

Too Many
Mouths to Feed

During the ten days the delegates at the World Food Conference argued about how to fight starvation, the birth of 2 million more earthlings aggravated the crisis.

"I hear the dreadful ticking of the biological clock," declared Norman Borlaug. "Five births occur every two seconds. That means over 70 million new mouths to feed every year. To put it another way, a new nation the size of the United States or Russia is now appearing on earth every three years."

The population explosion is a domestic as well as a foreign problem for Americans. David E. Lilienthal, chairman of the Development and Resources Corporation, a private firm, warned that the expected 300 million population of the United States by the year 2000 will bring a taxpayers' revolt. With computer technology making human labor more and more superfluous, treasury costs will grow astronomical for unemployment benefits, food subsidies, welfare, and social security, to say nothing of expanded public services, schools, hospitals, and water purification and antipollution measures.

"By the year 2000," Lilienthal predicted, "the high cost of breathing will be a real issue, not just a phrase." The *Statistical Abstract of the United States* reveals that the life expectancy of the average American has already declined by five months since 1966 because of food, water, and air pollution causing destruction of the environment.

Roger Revelle, director of Harvard's Center for population Studies, estimated that by the middle of the next century some of today's cities may have become a hundred times larger than they already are now.

The shadow of coming events may have been cast in Calcutta, where one out of five of its residents—600,000 people—live, eat, and sleep in the streets, lying on the ground like bundles of rags. Women huddle over piles of animal manure, patting it into cakes for fuel. Children compete with dogs for garbage. Those who survive grow into ragged skeletons, barefoot, hollow-eyed, apathetic.

Yet more and more thousands crowd to the big coastal cities of India from overflowing villages where the land no longer produces enough food, hoping for handouts from American grain ships.

There are more than 500 million people in India today. By the end of the century there may well be one billion.

The world statistics are staggering. There are now 65 per cent more people on earth than there were only thirty years ago. Of all people who have ever lived on the planet, one in twenty-five is now alive and requiring food.

At the outset of the Christian era, the whole world had only 250 million people. If the rate of increase had remained fixed at the level of that day, it would have taken another 1,600 years to double the population. Today the population is expected to double in another thirty-five years.

"A child born today, living on into his seventies, would

These Nigerian babies are officially described as being "in less serious stages of malnutrition." (UNICEF/POUL LARSEN)

know a world of 15 billion," pointed out Robert McNamara. "His grandson would share the planet with 60 billion. . . . India, for example, is adding a million a month to its population."

According to the Economic Commission for Asia and the Far East, Asia's population will double by the end of the century. It will then have more people than are alive today in the entire world.

"Every day the equivalent of twenty divisions of Martians invade this planet without their field rations," observed Lord Ritchie Calder, noted British scientist. *New York Times* columnist James Reston wrote somberly, "The political and social implications of human fertility are only dimly realized."

The largest birth rate is in Asia, Africa, and Latin America, where most people live at bare subsistence levels. The average number of children per family in those areas is five. Poverty and large families go hand in hand. In the United States poor families represent only about one-eighth of the population but account for one-fourth of the nation's birth rate.

Two out of every five people alive today in the poorer nations are under fifteen years old. As they mature and marry, they will produce the greatest baby boom of all time. "Those youngsters," wrote Paul R. Ehrlich in his book *The Population Bomb*, "are the reason for all the ominous predictions for the year 2000. They are the gunpowder for the population explosion."

Rapidly spreading malnutrition, however, may curb this expansion. "In at least a dozen countries and perhaps as many as twenty, death rates that had been declining are turning sharply upward," reported Lester R. Brown of the Overseas Development Council, a nonprofit organization in Washington, D.C. The diseases checked by modern epidemiology are once more threatening millions whose bodies are too ravaged by undernourishment to resist.

But if the world goes on doubling its numbers every thirty-five years, by the end of the next century there will be 60,000 *trillion* people on earth—100 for every square yard of the globe, land, or sea. The only possible way they could exist, suggested British physicist J. H. Fremlin, would be vertically, in a continuous 2,000-story-high building that would cover the planet.

The key factor in the equation between breeding and feeding is the rate of acceleration of both. Unless food supplies can keep pace with population growth, catastrophe is inevitable. Unfortunately, we do not know how to increase food at the rate at which people multiply.

It took millions of years before our planet acquired its first billion people. But it took less than 100 years to acquire its second billion. And it took less than 30 years to acquire its third billion. A fourth billion will be here in just half *that* time.

"It is clear," Henry Kissinger warned at the Rome Conference, "that population cannot continue to double indefinitely every generation."

By prolonging lives on an individual basis through modern technology, we may only be dooming collective human life to extinction by overpopulation. To multiply food, homes, roads, transport facilities, hospitals, schools, and jobs at the same rate as the population explosion would require a staggering effort in the United States. For the poor countries of the world, the task would be impossible.

Many Americans do not consider the United States obligated to give food aid to those hungry nations which continue to multiply their number without restraint. "The more we feed," protested conservationists Robert and Leona Train Rienow, "the more they breed."

Food production must keep pace with population growth. (GENE BASSET, SCRIPPS-HOWARD NEWSPAPERS)

Zero Population Growth, Inc., an organization dedicated to holding the world's numbers where they are, takes the unsentimental view that every child saved in Southeast Asia, India, or Africa will eventually bring forth children of his or her own to live in even greater misery. "The problem is not that there is too little food," declared ZPG spokesman Johnson C. Montgomery. "The problem is there are too many people—many too many. . . . We have mindlessly tried to cram too many of us into too short a time span. Four billion humans are fine—but they should have been spread over several hundred years." Worried that the United States might weaken itself drastically by dividing up all its food reserves with the rest of the world, he asked, "Should we eat the last tuna fish, the last ear of corn, and utterly destroy the garden?" Such views anger people in the hungry nations, who consider it elitist and racist of Americans to urge birth control on them; some brand it a form of attempted genocide.

Also opposing these views are most church organizations of the United States, which hold that Americans must, indeed, be their brothers' keepers. While agreeing that Americans must look after their own needy, they consider that the United States can also well afford to make substantial contributions toward ending world hunger.

"We would be failing in our Christian duty if we closed our hearts to the suffering cries of these helpless people," declared Dr. W. Stuart McBirnie, president of the Community Churches of America. Deploring the failure of the World Food Conference to provide sufficient aid at once to the starving nations, he urged Americans to join fasts and send the money saved to food relief agencies.

More than sacrifice on the affluent nations, however, will be needed to solve the basic problem. By world standards it takes one acre of arable land to feed one person. But each new person added to the population requires a fifth of an acre of "paved land"—land taken out of agriculture for homes, roads, factories, and other support purposes. Paradox: How can more food be grown for new diners at the global table when each new mouth that must be fed reduces the available land needed for farming?

Overpopulation, warned Robert McNamara, is the greatest single obstacle to feeding the world's poor and giving them the hope of a better life. At the present rate of births, he reminded us, "in six and a half centuries from now—the same insignificant period of time separating us from the poet Dante—there would be one human being standing on every square foot of land on earth: a fantasy of horror that even the *Inferno* could not match."

But a more immediate horror looms ahead in the very near future. If population growth goes uncontrolled, millions of babies born all over the world today, tomorrow, and next year will be condemned to starvation and disease.

Because we simply can't grow food fast enough.

4

We Can't Grow Food Fast Enough

The romantic views of French philosopher Jean Jacques Rousseau had a large following in the latter part of the eighteenth century. Rousseau argued that if only man would return to nature, and share the earth's wealth equally, society could be blissful. A friend and disciple, English squire Daniel Malthus, sought to convert his son Thomas to Rousseau's views.

But the thirty-one-year-old clergyman's training as an economist made him skeptical. It was impossible to create a contented society on earth, Thomas Malthus insisted, simply because the population increased faster than the food supply. Population jumped in a geometric progression (2-4-8-16-32-64), while food increased only in an arithmetic progression (2-4-6-8-10-12).

It always took a major disaster, such as famine, war, or pestilence, to restore the balance temporarily. But then the cycle would begin all over again until its next check by mass deaths. There could be no hope for humanity, because at the end of each century there would only be a third as much food for each person on earth as at its beginning, until people agreed to reduce the birth rate by "moral restraint."

Malthus published his views in 1798 as *An Essay on the Principle of Population as it affects the Future Improvement of Society*. The Malthusian theory excited wide controversy, and has been hotly debated ever since its promulgation. It was decried by church and political leaders opposed to limiting population. When Malthus' prophecy of impending doom failed to materialize during the nineteenth century, critics dismissed him as an unscientific alarmist. His defenders insisted that catastrophe had only been delayed by vast immigration to the New World, which had only a tiny population and tremendous natural wealth to exploit.

The passing years did not bear out Malthus' dire predictions, but the recurrence of a population explosion and growing world hunger in our own time has revived interest in his basic assumptions. Malthus could not have foreseen the growth of agricultural science, which has vastly increased crops through modern farm machinery and technology. But while this development has eased the dilemma, it has not solved it. Few of the world's small farmers are able to use this technology. Most continue to work the soil the way their ancestors did.

Rice paddies in China have been worked the same way for centuries. (FAO/H. HENLE)

The U.S. Science Advisory Committee to the President reported that the rate of growth in food production of the underdeveloped countries in 1967 was less than half the growth of their population. This ratio has placed an impossible burden on their farms, which cannot feed the increased population and cannot even employ them as agricultural workers. During the 1960's, consequently, 130 million people were forced to migrate from rural to urban areas, causing severe unemployment problems. The FAO has warned that as many as another 170 million might have to migrate before 1980.

"In the developing world . . . malnutrition affects some 400 million people; a less conservative definition might double the figure," reported Sayed Ahmed Marei, secretary-general of the World Food Conference. He urged that this figure be understood not just as a "cold statistic," but as "the daily physical privation of fellow human beings, adversely affecting health and physical growth and seriously reducing the capacity of children to learn and adults to work."

Some poorer countries export agricultural produce, even though their own people are hungry, because they need the money to buy other imports. In order to earn dollar credits, some must use their soil for single-export crops like sugar cane or bananas.

The ability of the richer countries to help with surplus foods lessens as their cities expand to accommodate population growth. In North America, Europe, and Japan housing developments, shopping centers, and recreational facilities are replacing fields of wheat, corn, and rice.

If this trend continues, in North America particularly, the consequences could be grave for most of the world's people, who depend upon these grains for survival. The fertile lands of the United States and Canada comprise the only major source of surplus cereal exports, supplying 91 out of the 97 million tons shipped annually.

This California housing development is built on land that once was a fruit orchard. (WIDE WORLD PHOTOS)

The problem of world food shortages is complicated by the special food needs and taboos of various cultures. Some Americans resent the shipment of free or cheap wheat to hungry India because of that country's enormous number of sacred cows, which the Indians refuse to slaughter for food.

One of the problems of shipping surplus foods to famine-stricken countries is that they are not always suitable. Condensed or powdered milk is sometimes sent to hungry Third World people who have developed, early in life, an intolerance to the lactose in cow's milk. Unable to tolerate any milk product but low-sugar yogurt, they become further weakened by dehydration and diarrhea, and many die.

Specialized food needs of people are another reason why the FAO believes that emphasis must be placed on helping poor countries supply their own needs, rather than keeping them dependent on imports of foreign food. But the task of producing enough homegrown food to keep up with the expanding population is difficult even for successful agricultural countries like China. In 1975, with 860 million Chinese to feed, Premier Chou En-lai felt compelled to call for a "comprehensive modernization" of Chinese agriculture.

The Malthusian ratio seems to be working against many of the poorer nations. After an absence of ten years, Lord Ritchie Calder revisited Java, which had managed to increase its crops by 25 per cent in the interval.

He found chronic famine persisting: "I saw the prevalence of marasmus, the working skeletons; of hunger edema; of kwashiorkor, the children with rusted hair and skins cracked like a crazy-paving; the xerophthalmia, the blindness of vitamin deficiency and infants dehydrated by hunger. . . . And why? Because while the food production had increased by 25 per cent in ten years, the population had increased by 30 per cent. And that 5 per cent difference meant hunger in all its gradations from malnutrition to starvation."

People who subsist largely on fish diets have seen supplies of this protein source dwindle with the growing demand for food. Herring have virtually disappeared from the North Sea and the Atlantic coast of Europe. Sardine schools are so diminished off South America that it doesn't pay fishermen to go after them. Haddock has grown so scarce that commercial fishermen are now forbidden to take them off the American Atlantic coast. Many species of fish and shellfish have been harvested past their ability to replace themselves.

Even normally optimistic industry spokesmen are worried. "It's kind of frightening," admitted David H. Wallace, associate administrator of the National Ocean Industries Association.

Ocean pollution has aggravated the problem. "With my own two eyes I have seen the oceans sicken," declared Captain Jacques Yves Cousteau, the French oceanographer. "Certain reefs that teemed with fish only ten years ago are now almost lifeless. The ocean bottom has been raped by trawlers. . . . And everywhere are sticky globs of oil, plastic refuse and unseen clouds of poisonous affluents."

He added, "Remember when the inexhaustible sea, so-called, was going to feed all the world's new billions? Four years ago I knew that the amount of life in the oceans was dwindling at a terrifying rate. Yet I predicted that the fishing tonnage would continue to rise for a few years because of better equipment methods—and I was wrong. The tonnage of fish started down in 1971 and has kept going down ever since."

Fish harvests are further threatened by countries seeking to exploit the ocean for oil and mineral products. "Do you want to fish, or do you want to mine?" Elisabeth Mann Borgese asked them in her book, *The Drama of the Oceans.* ". . . For if you want to fish where you want to mine, there'll be no fish. The shock of seismic explosions, the drilling and the spilling will kill or drive them off. . . . The trouble is that frequently the oil is where the fish are."

On sea or land we find an inability of food production to keep up with soaring populations. Spacecraft earth is overloaded.

"The American dream, based as it is on the concept of unlimited space and resources, is withering away," declared Nathaniel P. Reed, assistant secretary of the interior for fish and wildlife and parks. "The earth as a place to live has a limited amount of air, water, soil, minerals, space and other natural resources—and today we are pressing hard on our resource base."

In 1961 the world had enough grain reserves to feed the earth's population for another ninety-four days. By mid-1974 growth in the world's numbers had shrunk these reserves to only a twenty-nine-day supply. Norman Borlaug analyzed the danger:

"There is less than a one per cent margin of reserves left in the world food grain supply . . . less than a one per cent

However, how and distribute ???

)r error before untold millions of people starve to
e disaster that faces us can come in almost any
ghts in Africa or Russia, too much rain in India
_ast Asia, a plant disease such as rust infestation in
America."

Many poor nations, making heroic efforts to increase their own food supplies, blame the rich nations for monopolizing an unfair share of the world's food and resources. They point out that North Americans constitute 6 per cent of the people on earth, yet consume 40 per cent of the world's resources. In the United States and Canada, each person accounts for one ton of grain a year—1,800 pounds of it in the form of feed for cattle and poultry. Consequently the agricultural resources—land, water, fertilizer—used to feed one North American are almost five times as great as those used to provide grain for one Nigerian or Peruvian.

The minimum diet for avoiding malnutrition is 2,300 calories per day, including two and a half ounces of protein. More than half the people in the world today subsist on fewer than 2,000 calories a day, and their diet is mostly protein-deficient.

When the hungry nations of the Sahel asked for emergency food to ease their famine in 1974, they were belatedly sent a total of a million tons of grain. That year the world's rich countries fed 400 times as much grain to their livestock. Common Market countries, to hold down beef prices, gave their farmers a subsidy of surplus wheat as animal feed, stained red so that it could not be used for human consumption.

In the United States, between 1967 and 1972, the government paid almost $10 billion in subsidies to farmers for corn crops used to feed livestock. Cattle were also fed large amounts of soymeal, a high-quality source of protein. Yet cattle and sheep can thrive on grass and forage. They were fed crops instead because grain-fed cattle and sheep provide fat-marbled, tenderer meat. Millions of Americans enjoyed juicier dinners. Millions of the world's poor went hungry.

Critics accuse us of showing more concern for our domestic pets than we do for needy humanity. The pet industry sold well over $2 billion worth of cat and dog food to pet owners in 1974, consuming millions of tons of meat, poultry, seafood, and feed grains. Much of it is highly nutritious wheat germ, wheat bran, and soymeal. "You could feed 7 million human beings a complete diet with what goes into dog and cat food," observed Dr. Alan Beck of New York's Bureau of Animal Affairs.

To feed our 5 million riding horses we use 25 million acres of farmland that could otherwise grow crops for people. George Allen, of the Department of Agriculture, pointed out that this lost grain could also mean lower livestock prices: "There is no question that the housewife's supermarket costs are higher because of pleasure horses."

American pets are better fed than millions of the world's people.
(NEW YORK PUBLIC LIBRARY PICTURE COLLECTION)

While poor countries suffer crop failures because of fertilizer shortages, we use fertilizer lavishly for non-food purposes. "The people of the United States," pointed out the *Nation*, "use as much fertilizer on their ornamental gardens as India employs to produce food—and our pets consume a high percentage of the globe's fish protein."

During an Indian famine, when John F. Kennedy was president, he offered the Indian government a small grain shipment along with funds for a population-control program, making it clear that the United States expected a reduction in the future number of Indian mouths to be fed. Outraged, the Indian ambassador to the United Nations promptly denounced the shipment as "unworthy of a fourth-rate power, let alone the most powerful nation on earth." The average American family dog, he declared, was fed more animal protein each week than the average Indian received in a month. "How do you justify taking fish from protein-starved Peruvians and feeding them to your animals?" he demanded. And he concluded bitterly, "I contend that the birth of an *American* baby is a greater disaster for the world than that of twenty-five Indian babies!" The UN General Assembly passed a vote of condemnation of the United States.

Paul Ehrlich agreed with this viewpoint, observing, "Each American child is fifty times more of a burden on the environment than each Indian child."

British economist Barbara Ward found that about a third of the world's increased demand for food was the result of "stuffing by the affluent." Ecologist Barry Commoner noted in *Science and Survival*, "Every day we produce 11,000 calories of food per capita in the U.S. We need only 2,500 calories."

The amount of food we waste horrifies visitors from the world's poor regions. They observe the meat, bread, and butter left unfinished in restaurants and scraped into the garbage in homes. A California study released in January

1975 found that Americans waste almost $5 billion worth of food each year in spoiled meat, fruit, and vegetables, by carelessly buying too much at one time.

Americans resent being blamed for world hunger. Some point out that in poor countries the ruling classes often seek luxury for themselves, shrugging off the hunger of the masses. Why should Americans feel guilty about the foreign hungry when their own rulers so often exploit them cruelly?

It is easier to shut one's eyes to mass hunger as long as the sufferers remain remote, unpersonalized statistics. But Winston Churchill once described what it was like to be brought face-to-face with a starving Asian mother and child:

"This year, for the first time, I was confronted with mass starvation at first hand. The horror of seeing a young child, its limbs withered to the diameter of a broom handle and its belly grossly distended to the size of a pregnant woman's, in the final and prolonged agonies of death by starvation is something impossible to forget. . . . I also recall my feelings of shame and helplessness as, empty-handed, I turned my back and walked away, knowing that in a few short days I should be back in England, a land of plenty, and that neither she nor her baby would live to see another Christmas unless help came urgently."

Even if the rich nations felt total compassion for the plight of the hungry nations, is it really within their power to end world starvation? One population expert estimated that if all the people on earth were to share the present global food supply equally, we would *all* starve to death.

As for feeding the population of the future, Paul Ehrlich declared that by A.D. 2000 the world's present food production would have to double. And that, as agricultural consultant Dr. William Paddock had pointed out in his book *Famine 1975! America's Decision, Who Will Survive?*, is flatly impossible.

The United States will have to choose which countries it

will feed, Paddock predicted, a decision which would undoubtedly be based on political considerations. Some Americans urge applying the concept of triage, which holds that in desperate emergencies aid must be rationed and only those capable of benefitting from help should be offered it. Applying this concept, first propounded by battlefront surgeons in World War I, to the problem of hunger, these people believe that food aid is wasted if it is sent either to a nation strong enough to recover without it or to one so weak that its people will perish anyhow, even with the aid.

The emergency of starvation is just the most visible part of a greater problem, warned UN's World Health Organization (WHO). Only a small number of the total world population actually starve to death. But billions of people awaken, work, and go to bed constantly hungry and undernourished, weakened by the sicknesses that prey on malnutrition.

We need a clearer appreciation of the kind of living death that billions on earth endure because they get only enough food to keep them barely alive.

5
The Half-Deaths
of Hunger

Dr. Derrick B. Jelliffe was puzzled. Visiting a Uganda mountain village from the Makerere University of East Africa where he was a UNICEF Professor of Pediatrics and Child Health, he could not account for the strikingly different appearances of a woman's two children. The infant at her breast looked well-fed and healthy. But her two-year-old, Bakumi, had bone-thin arms, sparse copper-colored hair, a distended belly above which ribs rippled like a washboard, and swollen feet.

Seeking an explanation, Dr. Jelliffe learned that for Bakumi's first six months or so he, too, had been contented and healthy feeding at his mother's breast. But when his mother had become pregnant again, Bakumi had been weaned abruptly, as a local custom required. Then he had been forced to subsist on the local staple food, cassava, a poor source of both protein and calories.

Cut off from protein-rich breast milk, Bakumi was also deprived of the psychological comfort of nursing. He grew melancholy and irritable. Weakened by malnutrition, he suffered a series of infections including whooping cough, recurrent malaria, and roundworms. When Dr. Jellife saw him, the symptoms of vomiting, diarrhea, fever, and poor appetite indicated the first stages of kwashiorkor, the disease caused by protein and nutritional deficiency.

Dr. Jelliffe found Bakumi's urban equivalent in a hospital in a Southeast Asian city. Eight-month-old David had the creased face and roughened skin of a wrinkled old man. Dr. Jelliffe learned that his mother had been feeding him a powdered milk formula. To stretch out the milk she could barely afford, she had diluted it beyond the point of nourishment with water from an infected source. Inevitably, the baby had come down with marasmus, the disease caused by lack of food calories, as well as debilitating diarrhea.

"The picture of malnutrition seen in young children throughout the world is essentially that of Bakumi and baby David multiplied a millionfold," stated Dr. Jelliffe.

In a 1974 study of nutrition in the Sahel region of Africa, the U.S. Center for Disease Control (CDC) found between 10 to 20 per cent of the children aged six months to six years severely and acutely undernourished. In countries beset by fighting as well as drought, disruption of food supplies brings death to vast numbers quickly. After the Nigerian civil war, one observer reported, "One hardly sees children aged between six months and five years."

The first victims claimed by epidemics are always the undernourished. In 1879 British barrister Cornelius Walford, in a study of *Famines of the World,* wrote: "It has been a common observation that in many epidemics the fever has raged among the poor in a degree proportionate to the privations they have endured. It was especially observable during the Irish potato famine: those persons who had been reduced by insufficient food were invariably attacked."

It is difficult for the privileged to have any real appreciation of what it feels like to be chronically hungry. Describing his experiences with near-starvation in *Down and Out in Paris and London,* George Orwell wrote that he found himself unable to pass any shop displaying food:

"Everywhere there is food insulting you in huge, wasteful piles; whole dead pigs, baskets of hot loaves, great yellow blocks of butter, strings of sausages, mountains of potatoes. . . . A sniveling self-pity comes over you at the sight of so much food. You plan to grab a loaf and run, swallowing it before they catch you; and you refrain, from pure funk."

Orwell lacked the energy to get out of bed for longer than half a day at a time, and was unable to interest himself in anything: "Only food could rouse you. You discover that a man who has gone even a week on bread and margarine is not a man any longer, only a belly with a few accessory organs. . . . Hunger reduces one to an utterly spineless, brainless condition, more like the after-effects of influenza than anything else. It is as though one had been turned into a jellyfish, or as though all one's blood had been pumped out and lukewarm water substituted. Complete inertia is my chief memory of hunger."

In the underdeveloped nations of the world, three out of five people go to bed hungry every night. In Africa, the Far East, and the Near East, people subsist on up to 10 per cent fewer calories, and 60 per cent less protein, than the minimum needed to avoid malnutrition.

According to FAO estimates, "Ten million of the children under five years of age in the developing countries are suffering from severe malnutrition, 80 million from moderate malnutrition, and 120 million from less obvious, milder forms of malnutrition. In total, therefore, about half of all the children in the developing world may be inadequately nourished."

WHO investigators Ruth Rice Puffer and Carlos V. Serrano found that in some Latin American countries more than

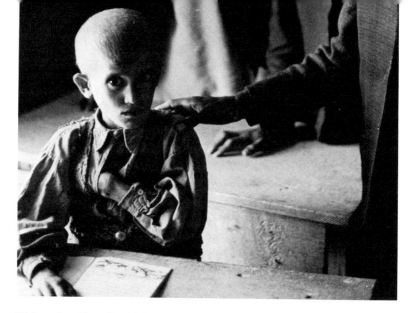

This schoolboy in Afghanistan, like most of his classmates, told UNICEF agents that he had been eating grass. (UNICEF/JOHN BALCOMB)

half the deaths of children under five are the result, directly or indirectly, of nutritional deficiencies.

More than 400 million people, the FAO noted, have too little food to meet the energy requirements of their work. Many suffer from vitamin A deficiency, nutritional anemia, and endemic goiter. The FAO pointed out that while dramatic cases of famine "rightly attract world-wide attention, they should not obscure the fact that most deaths from malnutrition result from a long-term deficiency of food that goes virtually unnoticed in conditions that pass for 'normal.'" Malnourished people may look normal, but their body tissues are often deficient in essential nutrients.

Many of the world's poor subsist on a diet made up largely of cheap starchy foods, which ironically fatten them while leaving them malnourished. Asked about hunger among the black poor in Mississippi in 1967, Governor Paul Johnson replied scornfully, "All the Negroes I've seen around here are so fat they shine!" But serious malnutrition is a problem of the poor in the United States, as it is elsewhere.

In a National Nutrition Survey, HEW found that 7 million

children of the American poor lagged as much as two and a half years behind well-nourished children in physical development. A third were also weak and apathetic because of nutritional anemia and shortages of vitamins A and C. "We've found more malnutrition than I ever expected to see in a society described as the best fed in the world," declared Dr. Arnold Schaefer. He added, "It is . . . shocking to realize that the problems in the poverty groups in the United States seem to be very similar to those we have encountered in the developing countries."

A study reported by the American Association for the Advancement of Science revealed that even when hungry children are brighter than well-fed children, they tend to fall behind the well-fed group intellectually by the age of three.

"Children who have been malnourished for more than the first four months," reported the University of Colorado Medical Center, "do not 'catch up' in physical or mental development." The handicaps of hunger are permanent.

Lack of protein in infancy, particularly during the first eighteen months of a baby's life, can inflict lifetime damage on the nervous system, even causing mental retardation. By the age of four the brain has already achieved 90 per cent of its growth. Studies of Mexican, South American, African, Egyptian, Indian, and Japanese children indicate that lack of proper food has stunted brain development in 10 to 25 per cent.

An FAO study, presented to the World Food Conference in Rome, showed that to prevent this tragedy would require only $20 a year per child, for an additional supplement of 600 calories and 20 grams of protein to the daily diet of the world's hungry children. Accordingly, a total ten-year appropriation of $500 million — less than the cost of one new bomber — could prevent the ravages of child malnutrition.

The half-deaths of hunger may turn into full deaths for children more often than we realize. Death certificates may certify pneumonia, influenza, or some other immediate cause, but seldom identify the basic condition responsible for making the victim vulnerable—semi-starvation.

In a two-year study of four Guatemalan villages, 222 deaths of infants under four had been listed officially as caused by worms. But researchers found that at least 40 per cent of these victims had shown symptoms of kwashiorkor. Worms alone would not have taken the lives of properly nourished infants.

The inadequate nutrition of pregnant women is as serious a problem as that of infants. Doctors consider it the reason why the United States ranks only thirteenth in the world in safe childbirths. Poorly fed mothers-to-be often have prematurely born babies. "Preemies" not only have lower resistance to infection but also more learning problems.

"The premature birth rate of the poor," Dr. Charles Upton Lowe, scientific director of the National Institute of Child Health, told Congress, "is three times that of the well-to-do. As many as 50 per cent of prematurely born infants grow to maturity with intellectual capacity significantly below normal. The children of the poor show impaired learning ability three to five times as often as other children."

Thus, malnutrition and its attendant miseries are passed on from hungry mothers to hungry infants.

Commonly lacking in the diet of the poor is vitamin A, the absence of which can cause blindness, a severe problem in India, Indonesia, Bangladesh, Vietnam, the Philippines, northeast Brazil, and El Salvador. In the Far East alone, more than 100,000 children go blind each year because of a vitamin A deficiency.

Anemia caused by lack of iron in the diet afflicts up to 15 per cent of the men and 35 per cent of the women in Latin American countries. Pregnant women and babies up to eighteen months are most susceptible especially those with hookworm, an infection that parasitizes what little iron may be in the diet. Another serious problem of malnutrition is goiter, accompanied by mental and physical retardation.

When Rockefeller Foundation scientist Frank Byrnes went to Colombia, he quickly found the dry statistics of malnutrition translated into heartbreaking reality. There was, for example, ragged nine-year-old Ana Ruth, who did not realize that her aunt had brought her to the hospital to die in comfort, two weeks after her younger brother had died at home.

Ana Ruth's belly was bloated, her legs swollen, her hair turning reddish and brittle—classic signs of kwashiorkor. Her condition was aggravated by the pneumonia that frequently overtakes victims of the disease.

A kind doctor gave the barefoot girl a pair of new dark blue sneakers, the first shoes she had ever owned. Fearful that the staff might take them away, Ana Ruth wore them in her hospital bed day and night. The sympathetic staff made no objection as they nursed her for pneumonia. Feeding her a minimum-level protein diet, they watched the sodium-potassium balance in her system carefully to avoid the risk of sudden death from the additional strain on her heart.

Ana Ruth lost over two pounds of water a day for three days, and her body swelling abated. Her reddish hair fell out as a new growth of black hair began to sprout. Narrowly escaping her brother's fate, Ana Ruth made it back home, proudly wearing her precious new sneakers. She was one of the lucky ones . . . temporarily. Until the lack of nutritious food made her belly and legs begin to swell once more.

Where drought and famine strike, disease is quick to follow. In the Sahel "obsolete" diseases like scurvy, beri-beri, and rickets reappeared in refugee camps and small towns.

Dr. Ibrahima Konate, executive director of a seven-nation organization coordinating projects in the Sahel, warned that the drought would "affect the children in the area even four or five years from now. Maybe our countries will find that they have unusual numbers of handicapped people."

The half-deaths of hunger have tragic consequences for

both victims and society, on our own country as well as overseas. Reporting on his study of malnourished Americans, Dr. Robert Coles of the Harvard University Health Services declared: "I am afraid that these parents and children do, indeed, become what some of their harshest and least forgiving critics call them: listless, apathetic, hard to understand, disorderly, subject to outbursts and self-injury and destructive violence toward others . . . I fear I am talking about millions of psychological catastrophes."

Malnourished children grow up "out of sight and ignored," according to a team of physicians who were sent to rural Mississippi in 1967 by the Field Foundation to study hunger. The doctors were appalled when child after child they examined proved to be suffering from vitamin and mineral deficiencies, severe anemia, and diseases caused by malnutrition. "We saw children," they reported, "whose nutritional and medical condition we can only describe as shocking —even to a group of physicians whose work involves daily confrontation with disease and suffering." The children lacked "the energy and ability to live a normally active life."

Many educators today are aware that children once

An American family, living in their pickup truck. (WIDE WORLD PHOTOS)

assumed to be stupid and lazy in class may simply be manifesting symptoms of chronic malnutrition. Principal W. P. Phipps of Davy, West Virginia, reported what happened when federal food aid to the school district was increased by a third:

"I have seen boys and girls come to school hundreds of times without food. . . . These pupils were undernourished and as a result they were listless and dull in school. Those in school whose parents were not on relief vastly outshone the others in school work and other activities. Since the Food Stamp Program has come to our county, I have found this to have changed immensely. . . . The people who receive the food stamps have been able to have such a variety in their diets that the children have become more alert in school and can hold their own with the rest in their academic work. They are no longer listless and without hope."

Some educationalists believe that money for special remedial or enrichment classes for underprivileged children would be better spent in making certain that they are not too hungry to learn. What may need enrichment most is not their curriculum but their diets. The Black Panthers acted on this belief during the 1960's by organizing free breakfasts for ghetto children.

"It has been noted time and again that when a hot lunch is offered to disadvantaged children," Rodger Hurley observed in his book, *Poverty and Mental Retardation,* "many of those who were previously . . . drowsy and largely uneducable become alive, alert and involved in the classroom situation."

Studies show that people who were severely malnourished as children score an average of thirteen points lower on IQ tests than those who were not, are much more likely to have damaged nervous systems, and are invariably shorter.

The half-deaths of hunger are also costly to a nation because they incapacitate millions for work, making them burdens on society. Dr. Charles Upton Lowe told Congress, "The ill-fed among 7 million poor American children constitute a danger to the nation, for they may never function in the labor market."

Nutritional diseases abounded in what were known as the Hungry Hills of central Java, where the people were forced to live on coconuts, bananas, and cassava. They were too debilitated to tackle a difficult project that would have given them rice—planting steep terraces and irrigating them by cutting a long canal through a volcanic ridge. To make the project possible, WHO and UNICEF sent teams into the Hungry Hills in 1955 to clear up the nutritional diseases of the Javanese. Soon afterward the people began building a crude coffer-dam at the headwaters of the Progo River, scurrying up swaying bamboo ladders with baskets of rubble on their heads. Gouging out the canal, they chipped away persistently at the volcanic rock with hammers and chisels, taking a year to progress two miles. "Isn't it a wonderful sight?" marveled a UN irrigation expert in 1962. When a UN observer suggested trying to get bulldozers for them, the expert exclaimed, "Don't you dare! Try to understand. This is *their* canal. For the first time they will have something they don't owe to the money-lenders!" Freed of energy-sapping nutritional diseases, there was now no work too arduous for the Javanese of the Hungry Hills.

"People who are sick cannot produce food nor earn the means to buy it," pointed out Lord Ritchie Calder. " . . . They succumb to the old litany of hunger: Better to walk than to run; better to sit than to walk; better to sleep than to sit; better to die than to sleep."

Some scientists consider it cruel to keep any people in the permanent half-death of hunger by helping them during a famine only to let them slip back again to the edge of starvation as soon as the crisis is over.

"Prolonging a few lives this year is of no avail," argued John D. Black in *Chronica Botanica,* "if this causes more misery and suffering in the years following. . . . Those who speak in this way are charged with being 'hard-boiled' and non-humanitarian, but they are the true humanitarians."

Church groups emphatically disagree, insisting that no one who cares about humanity can ignore the hungry. Many Americans who donate money to aid foreign victims of famine, however, ignore fellow Americans going hungry only a few blocks away. It is less upsetting to think of hunger in terms of Asia and Africa, half a world distant.

William H. Burson, director of Family and Children Services of Georgia, enumerated some of the Americans who refuse to recognize hunger in their backyards: "They are the county commissioner who maintains that his county cannot afford a food program. . . . They are the farmer or contractor looking for cheap labor who insists, 'if you feed them, they won't work.' They are the Sunday school teacher who piously quotes from the Scriptures that 'the poor always ye have with you'. . . . They are the well-fed businessman or banker who refuses to believe anyone is hungry because he never has been nor has he ever known anyone who has. They are the greedy merchant who charges he will be forced into bankruptcy if poor people are given food."

Ironically, these opponents of a crash program to end American malnutrition fail to recognize that the lack of it compels them to pay higher taxes. Reporting to the president in 1969, the Urban Affairs Council declared that it would cost only $457 a year to feed a poor child properly, while it was costing the government $1,516 a year for each malnourished child in welfare, hospitalization, and remedial and other expenses.

The real problem is not *whether* a government can afford to provide adequate nourishment for all its citizens, but *how*. For a while the United States and the rest of the world thought they had found the solution in the Green Revolution.

6

The
Green
Revolution

In 1726 Jonathan Swift wrote in *Gulliver's Travels,* "Whoever could make two ears of corn or two blades of grass to grow upon a spot of ground where only one grew before, would deserve better of mankind . . . than the whole race of politicians put together."

Almost 250 years later, in 1970, the Nobel Peace Prize was awarded to an American agricultural scientist, Dr. Norman Borlaug, for his unselfish and persistent labors to provide more food for the hungry people of the world by developing new strains of high-yield, disease-resistant wheat and taking them to the far ends of the earth to teach poor farmers how to grow them. His accomplishments won him worldwide renown as "the father of the Green Revolution."

As a young man at the University of Minnesota College of Agriculture in the 1930's, Borlaug had come under the influence of Dr. Elvin C. Stakman, head of the department of plant pathology. Stakman was a pioneer in research on crop rust, a disease caused by a parasitic fungus characterized by reddish-brown spots on leaves or stems. It could wipe out whole crops in a matter of days. Stakman sought to develop rust-resistant species of crops by cross-pollinating the least affected plants. It was an endless task because there were many types of rust, with new varieties constantly emerging.

In 1940, the Mexican government, whose crop yields were so low that it had to import half its food from the United States, asked Washington for help in increasing its wheat, corn, and bean yields. Vice President Henry A. Wallace was sympathetic, but knew that Congress would never vote funds to help a foreign country grow more corn and wheat while American granaries bulged with surpluses to sell.

Summoning representatives of the Rockefeller Foundation to his office, he told them that if they could help Mexico increase its food yield per acre, the Foundation would be contributing far more to the welfare of the Mexican people than they were with any of their other programs to promote world health and well-being.

In 1941, the Foundation dispatched Dr. Stakman and two other agricultural scientists to evaluate Mexico's farm problem. They found Mexican wheat varieties low in yield, genetically impure, and subject to crop rust. Plant pathologist J. George Harrar, a Stakman assistant, was selected to set up an Office of Special Studies in Mexico City. Here Dr. Harrar began organizing research, as well as training young Mexican agronomists in American agricultural techniques.

Norman Borlaug, who had been experimenting with rust in cereal grains under Dr. Stakman, was sent to an agricultural station at Chapino in 1944 to develop special cereal strains which would perform well in Mexico.

"These places I've seen have clubbed my mind—they are so poor and depressing," he wrote his wife. "The earth is so lacking in life force; the plants just cling to existence. They don't really grow; they just fight to stay alive. Nourishment levels are so low that wheat plants produce only a few grains, and even the weeds and diseases lack the food to be aggressive. No wonder the people are the way they are!"

For his experimental plots, Borlaug selected wheat plants which seemed disease-resistant and had a rich yield of kernels, replanting them for cross-fertilization. He had more than just Mexico in mind. Other hungry nations around the globe were also desperately seeking increased crop yields. Although the United States was the world's most successful food-growing nation, its technology was designed for a temperate climate and did not necessarily work when applied in tropical and subtropical zones.

Borlaug's first experimental plots of wheat were attacked by rust spores that spread rapidly to adjacent fields in warm, wet weather. He felt discouraged. Even if he could bring this strain of rust under control, there were more than 300 different known strains. Rust had destroyed half the Mexican grain harvest for three consecutive years.

Was his quest hopeless?

He tried again with four strains of rust-resistant wheat from Texas and Kenya, crossbreeding them with Mexican high-yield strains. When he had a few promising specimens, he traveled up and down the dusty central highlands of Mexico seeking to persuade skeptical farmers to try planting them.

Ill and miserable from unhygienic food and water in rural lodgings, Borlaug took to sleeping in barns, sheds, and under his truck, boiling his water. Persistent nausea and dysentery made him long for the comforts of laboratory work. But the sight of hungry Indian children, their bodies distorted by malnutrition, drove him on.

Like a seeker after the Holy Grail, he pursued the perfect wheat strain. Sweating in the fields under a blazing Aztec sun, he painstakingly transferred wheat pollen from stamen to pistil with tweezers, from dawn to dusk. By nightfall he was so bone-weary that he had barely enough energy left to

Norman Borlaug (center), with trainees at the Inter-American Wheat and Barley Program in Mexico. (FAO)

cook a can of food over a wood fire before he crawled into his sleeping bag and surrendered to exhaustion.

His Spartan physical labors appalled young Mexican agronomists in the program. Field work was for peons, not scientists. To perform it was to sacrifice one's social status. Why didn't Señor Borlaug simply give his plans to the experimental farm foreman, to be carried out by peon labor? Borlaug replied that the problem of hunger in Mexico was too urgent to be delayed by class divisions. Everyone must pitch in to grow more food for all. "Things must change," he warned. "You must work with the farmer and he must respect you! And you must work with the plants, you must know what you are growing."

But there was equal reluctance to cooperate on the part of Mexican farmers. They resisted change, resenting the young government agronomists as "book farmers." These university upstarts did not even know that one must use only wooden plows on the land because metal plows chilled the warmth and fertility of the earth!

Borlaug's first breakthrough, in the late 1940's, was the development of an experimental strain of rust-resistant, fast-growing wheat that would make possible two crops a year instead of just one. He set out to demonstrate the new seeds at an agricultural station in the Yaquí Valley.

But farmers in the valley, suspicious of Americans and skeptical of Borlaug's claims, refused to lend him a tractor, plow, disk harrow, or mule to help in sowing the demonstration crop. Undeterred, he located an old wooden hand cultivator in the station barn. Slipping into the harness, he pulled it through the station's fields himself, with the Mexican caretaker guiding the plow. Both men worked the fields with hand tools.

After three days a neighboring farmer finally took pity on the "crazy gringo" who had turned himself into a mule. He offered Borlaug the use of a small tractor and other farm implements over weekends. Gladly accepting, Borlaug continued to use hand tools on weekdays to get his planting done in time. He awaited the first crop anxiously.

The new wheat came up healthy, luxuriant, free of rust. Always the perfectionist, Borlaug patiently crossbred the strains by hand once more, achieving even stronger, more abundant crops. Now he sought to persuade the valley's farmers to test-grow the new seeds themselves.

They refused. The gringo might be able to play pretty tricks with nature at the experimental station, but who would be fool enough to risk one's own land, time, and harvest trying to imitate him? Especially since he used fertilizer. Everyone knew that made crops poisonous!

Borlaug persisted. Finally a farmer named Carlos Rodríguez consented to plant a bag of the seed, using the chemical fertilizer which Borlaug provided.

Two seasons later, when a raging outbreak of stem rust destroyed much of Mexico's wheat crop, Borlaug visited

Rodríguez' farm. He was mobbed and embraced by the farmer and his neighbors, who thanked him tearfully.

Rodríguez' first harvest with the new seeds had shown a 300 per cent increase in yield over any crops he had ever planted before. Keeping his promise to Borlaug, he had not sold or eaten any, replanting the seed instead and giving some to his neighbors. All had reaped a bountiful harvest. Their crops alone had remained untouched by the new rust blight that had ravaged other fields.

Borlaug happily reported the news to the first Latin American science conference held that summer in Mexico City. The Colombian government at once urged the Rockefeller Foundation to let Borlaug repeat his miracle for them. But he asked to remain with the Mexican project, eager to develop it on a large scale, and another agronomist went in his place.

In 1951 a new variety of rust attacked Mexican wheat, affecting some of Borlaug's strains as well. Once more he began painstakingly cross-fertilizing different types of wheat in search of a more disease-resistant hybrid. He developed one which was also heavier with kernels, but it grew too tall and slender, likely to topple before harvesting.

Borlaug now began experimenting with crosses of Japanese "dwarf" wheats, which had shorter, stronger straws. During 1952 he cultivated as many as 40,000 different wheat strains in his nurseries, the products of cross-fertilizing 6,000 species. The backbreaking work required that careful records be kept of every cross.

As he developed new rust-resistant, high-bearing strains, he persuaded Mexican farmers to test them in small, well-fertilized plots and compare the results with regular crops.

The first field tests were enormously successful, and the news spread rapidly. By 1955, thanks to Borlaug, Mexico had doubled its wheat grain harvest in just ten years, making it almost self-sufficient in grain.

But Borlaug knew that he was still in a race against time.

There were now 10 million more Mexicans to feed than there had been when he had first begun his work. And ten new virulent varieties of rust had appeared, threatening some of his semi-dwarf crosses. He kept at his massive crossbreeding experiments until he had developed new wheat strains uniquely better than any in the world.

New difficulties arose in the form of political pique. Many of the young Mexican agronomists, who were now contributing a great deal to the program, protested to their government that it was unfair to let the Americans run the show and take all the credit. The Mexican government decided to thank the Americans and invite their departure.

The news brought a storm of protest from Mexican farmers, who testified to all the wonders the Americans had performed for them. The government relented. Dr. Harrar soothed wounded Mexican pride by identifying the new dwarf wheat strains now being shipped to India and Pakistan as "Mexican wheat." He cautioned all American scientists in the program to maintain a low profile, putting on overalls and going to work in the fields as Borlaug did.

The controversy led the Rockefeller Foundation to change its policies. Curtailing its administrative functions abroad, it now sought to hew strictly to scientific work, training nationals to take over a program as soon as possible. The change also allowed the Foundation to offer help to more countries with severe hunger problems.

Borlaug continued crossing semi-dwarf wheat strains in search of ever more superior specimens. In 1960 one strain produced such a magnificent sample crop that his aide, Dr. Alfredo García, urged him not to wait until newer strains were perfected but to show it to local farmers. Against his judgment, Borlaug agreed.

Six truckloads of farmers visited the inspection point. Excited by what they saw, they swept Dr. García aside and raced into the plots to snatch seed heads. Station workers tried to hold them off and reclaim the grains, but the farmers fought back. Before the melee was over, jubilant farmers escaped with about a fifth of the new seed.

Borlaug acted promptly to prevent them from sowing it. What the farmers didn't know was that the bumper crop they had seen had one failing that hadn't been bred out of it yet—it made poor bread. Warning them, he offered free test varieties instead which made much better bread. The farmers gladly dumped the purloined seed and planted the other.

Borlaug's new semi-dwarf strains were so prolific that by 1963 they gave Mexico a crop six times greater than had been grown in 1944, and were used on 95 per cent of the nation's wheat lands. No longer an importer of flour grain, Mexico was now not only self-sufficient but had joined the United States and Canada as a wheat exporter. Seeds of the new Mexican strains were eagerly sought by Pakistan, India, Israel and other countries around the world.

The Green Revolution in Mexico held out great promise for all hungry nations because only a fifth of Mexico's land is suitable for growing crops; the rest consists of mountains, deserts, dry mesas, ranges, forests, and near-jungle. If such a food-deficit nation could be transformed into a food-surplus nation, eating 40 per cent more food than before the program had begun, why could not Borlaug's miracle be repeated all around the world?

World hopes were raised as the semi-dwarf strains of wheat were found to thrive equally as well abroad as in Mexico. Their ability to ripen quickly made them useful in cold climates with shorter growing seasons, and made multiple harvests possible in hot climates. The bread they produced was not as nutritious as American bread, but it was edible and the crops resisted most strains of rust.

Skeptical officials in some countries nevertheless refused to consider importing the Mexican seeds. Scientists at Turkish government research stations pronounced them unsuitable for local use. But one enterprising Turkish farmer, Mehmet Can Eliyesil, smuggled some into the country. Growing a bountiful, disease-resistant wheat crop, he demonstrated it to Turkish officials. The ban was lifted.

In less than one year, the number of world farmers using Mexican wheats increased from 100 to 50,000; within two years, to 200,000. The Green Revolution was aided by America's Agency for International Development. AID financed imports of needed fertilizer by the developing nations, and offered the services of 29,000 professional agriculturalists.

Borlaug's work with wheat spilled over into corn research. Aided by the Rockefeller Foundation, Mexico's plant geneticists developed fifty new basic types of corn. The new high yields soon provided even more food for Mexicans than the new wheat. Some strains have unprecedented resistance to drought and cold; others thrive at altitudes up to 10,000 feet; still others flourish in near-jungle lowlands. Consequently Mexican corn is also now growing in about eighty grain-hungry countries around the world.

Countries participating in the Green Revolution must use large applications of fertilizer to get the highest crop yields. Japan and Taiwan, heavy users, get up to four times the yield of Pakistan and India, which use relatively little. Most developing countries, unfortunately, have an acute shortage of fertilizer, which has become increasingly expensive since it is a derivative of high-priced oil and gas.

Farmers in regions where drought is common are encouraged to eliminate their dependence on rainfall by building tube wells. These cylindrical shafts driven into the ground, with water sucked up by electrical pumps, can be installed in just days or weeks. Unfortunately, the cost of $1,000 to $2,500 per tube well puts them beyond the reach of most poor farmers.

Borlaug's success with wheat led the Rockefeller Foundation to join with the Ford Foundation in 1962 to seek also a "miracle" rice strain by using his selective crossbreeding methods. Since 92 per cent of the world's rice crop is produced and eaten in Asia, a Rice Research Institute was established in the Philippines under Dr. Robert Chandler.

Scientists here were able to develop IR-8, a prolific short-stem, disease-resistant dwarf rice which, like the Mexican wheats, was able to double crop yields. After half a century of being forced to import rice, the Philippines grew so much that the country became an exporter. IR-8 is now being grown in Sri Lanka, Turkey, Burma, Malaysia, Indonesia, Afghanistan, Nepal, Laos and Vietnam. In addition to being highly adaptable to various climates, it matures in only 120 days, compared to up to 180 days for usual varieties, permitting farmers to harvest one extra crop a year.

Thanks to the Green Revolution, since 1948 world grain

Research on hybrid rice was also sponsored by the Food and Agriculture Organization of the United Nations in India. (FAO/ERIC SCHWAB)

production has soared by 103 per cent for wheat, 152 per cent for barley, 97 per cent for corn, 88 per cent for rice.

Unfortunately, world population has soared much faster.

On October 20, 1970, a phone call from Norway informed Norman Borlaug's wife that her husband had won the Nobel Peace Prize. It was awarded in Oslo on December 10, 1970, to the "indomitable man who fought rust and red tape . . . who, more than any other single man of our age, has provided bread for the hungry world . . . who has changed our perspective."

But in his acceptance speech, Borlaug warned, "The Green Revolution has not yet won the battle for food, because mankind is breeding too fast."

Some critics feel that the gain in food production, further-more, has been at the expense of the world's agricultural poor. "Increased productivity alone has not improved the lot of rural workers," pointed out Carlos Lleras Restrepo, former president of Colombia, in 1971, "but on the contrary frequently makes it worse." The gap has widened between poor and rich farmers because often only large landowners can afford to buy seed, fertilizer, and tube wells, and only they own the huge acreage to profit from big harvests.

"In India," Restrepo reported to the FAO, "the introduc-tion of new high-yield varieties had greatly reduced the immense deficits, but social tensions had increased."

In the *Atlantic Monthly,* Claire Sterling wrote in July 1975 that while the Green Revolution has doubled Indonesia's rice harvest, it has displaced over a million poor rural workers, who rioted in Jakarta in 1974. "More than half the smaller holdings in some parts of Java have already been swallowed up by larger farmers and newly rich absentee landlords; and experts predict that 80 per cent of the Javan population will be landless within just the next generation."

The shortage of high-priced fertilizer brought the Green Revolution to a halt in poor countries like India, which felt compelled to emphasize a return to traditional low-yield varieties of cereal needing less fertilizer.

The Green Revolution is not yet completed, and probably never can be even if fertilizer and irrigation cease to be problems. "While man breeds new wheats, nature breeds new rusts," Dr. Stakman pointed out in his book, *Campaigns Against Hunger,* "and occasionally she spawns virulent ones that can attack varieties that had been resistant to those previously prevalent."

The Green Revolution certainly deserves credit for bumper harvests in the developing countries between 1967 and 1970, but fortunate weather patterns helped. Despite the miracle strains of wheat, corn, and rice, drought and floods in subsequent years brought food shortages and famine.

Asked in 1974 whether he still believed that world food production could keep pace with population for the rest of the twentieth century, Borlaug replied: "I am no longer that optimistic. From 1947 until mid-1972, the world's consumption of food seemed stable. Then came the disastrous harvest of 1972, with a drought that swept across the Soviet Union, China, and Australia. That precipitated the big purchases of grain by Russia and triggered inflation. The same summer there were poor monsoon rains across all South Asia, and the rice crop was bad. Food reserves which we thought adequate to meet any situation simply disappeared overnight."

The Green Revolution nevertheless goes on, mankind's best hope for bigger harvests. International Minerals & Chemical Corporation, the world's largest private producer of fertilizers, is supporting food research in seven countries, and has sponsored twenty-two World Food Production Conferences throughout Asia and Latin America. Not without self-interest, IMC declared, "Among all the efforts to relieve the problems of world hunger, the revolutions in food production that can be achieved through fertilizers promise the most immediate relief."

The future of the Green Revolution may ultimately depend on the extent of the sacrifices people in the hungry countries are willing to make today for the sake of more food tomorrow, like those endured by the Russians and Chinese when they had to make over their starving societies earlier in this century.

During the Russian famine in 1921, American correspondent Raymond Swing observed a band of famished peasant refugees on the banks of the Volga near a mound of grain sacks guarded by a single Red soldier. He asked the white-bearded patriarch who led them why they didn't simply overpower the soldier, seize the sacks, and end their hunger. "That is seed grain," replied the patriarch. "We do not steal from the future."

7

Hunger
in India

October 1974. Tens of thousands of hungry Indians pour into the cities, swelling the slums of Calcutta and Bombay. The government is forced to open long food relief lines. All over the country men are abandoning wives and children to search for food. Some distraught fathers throw small children into rivers to end the burden of trying to feed them.

In rural regions of West Bengal 15 million people struggle to survive on 900 calories a day—1,400 under the bare minimum required for normal health.

Corpses lie for days in great numbers by roadsides or on railway platforms until they can be collected and removed for cremation. Most Indians die quietly, but some grow violent. Desperate mobs raid farmers for hoarded grain and attack freight trains suspected of carrying food. Within sight of the majestic Taj Mahal hungry peasants sack grain stores.

Drought in India, the calamity that undid the Green Revolution, wiped out its food reserves, and spread famine across the land. But even in the best of times, hunger is hardly a stranger to the average Indian, who subsists on only 400 pounds of cereal grain a year, compared to 2,000 pounds a year for the average American.

One of India's more progressive regions, Ajarpura, has a

Famine has always been part of India's history. This engraving of the 1870's depicts starving villagers at the shrine of the god Shiva's bull. (NEW YORK PUBLIC LIBRARY PICTURE COLLECTION)

death rate of 125 per 1,000 births, caused principally by malnutrition. *Science Journal* reported in May 1968 that nearly 80 per cent of Indian children were suffering from protein deficiency which permanently stunted their growth.

Some 4 million Indians are totally blind, and perhaps three times as many partially blind, because of vitamin A deficiencies. Up to a third of Indian mothers die in childbirth because of anemia. Nutrition is so poor that when India held Olympic trials in 1968, out of a population of 535 million people not a single Indian could qualify for *any* of the scheduled thirty-two track and field events.

Describing a New Delhi wedding for the *New York Times,* Ruth Prawer Jhabvala observed, "No one seems to notice that . . . at the front there is a rabble of children suffering from rickets and eye disease while at the back, where the waste food goes, a rabble of grownups is holding out old tins." Noting that Indians learn to ignore the hungry because they live in the midst of hunger all their lives, she explained, "It may be the reason why they eat so frenziedly, because when you have seen [hunger] for *that* long, you may be tempted to grab all you can while you can and help yourself with both hands."

When Norman Borlaug first visited India in 1952, he was stunned by the magnitude of the hunger problem and shocked by the primitive state of Indian agriculture. Before progress could be hoped for in underdeveloped nations, he reported, native young agronomists would have to be trained in practical techniques for increasing crop yields quickly.

At his suggestion, the Rockefeller Foundation funded such a project, the Mexican government made training facilities available, and the FAO selected candidates from South America, Afghanistan, Cyprus, Egypt, Ethiopia, Iran, Iraq, Jordan, Libya, Pakistan, Syria, Saudi Arabia, and Turkey. Ironically, at first India itself held apart from the program out of national pride. But when the other nations began showing remarkable increases in harvests, Indian agricultural scientists, too, began making their way to Mexico.

In the fall of 1963 India imported its first experimental semi-dwarf seeds, which were planted on a dozen acres. They thrived so vigorously that the enthusiastic teams of Mexican-trained Indian agronomists predicted a tenfold multiplication of the wheat yield. Despite difficulties in squeezing funds for fertilizer and farmer credit out of the government, the Green Revolution began to take root by the spring of 1964.

At the height of bumper crops in 1965, Indian officials were urged to set aside grain reserves in case of drought. "Why should we bother?" one replied. "Our reserves are the wheat fields of Kansas." The United States had been selling 2 million tons of wheat a year to India since 1951. It never occurred to New Delhi officials that the United States itself might suffer a drought, or that the drain on its reserves by drought-stricken countries might become too great.

Under pressure from Washington, India had begun to mechanize its agriculture. But by 1966 some 40 per cent of the nation's tractors were idle because of a lack of spare parts. Many other developing countries were experiencing the same difficulty, having bought obsolete farm equipment cheaply without regard for maintenance. When equipment had been purchased from several different countries, it was impossible to stock spare parts for all the different makes in use.

Erosion and overgrazing make much of India's land useless.
(FAO/H. NULL)

The Green Revolution could not control the weather. When India's monsoon rains failed to arrive in 1966, a terrible drought killed off millions of acres of wheat. Nothing grew. Indians also went thirsty as reservoirs dried up. In tens of thousands of villages, ponds became baked mud troughs and rats raced everywhere searching for grain. Children lay with eyes glazed, suffering from protein starvation. All of northeast India was declared a disaster area.

Riots broke out in the cities as students attacked government buildings with rocks. New Delhi officials appealed to U.S. ambassador Chester Bowles for help. But President Lyndon B. Johnson was irked with India for having sought to improve relations with North Vietnam, which he was in the midst of bombing. Despite his lip service to "fighting hunger in India," food aid shipments were meager and slow.

"It is a cruel performance," Bowles noted in his diary. "The Indians must conform; they must be made to fawn; their pride must be cracked. . . . The impression developed that the United States was more interested in . . . forcing a change in India's foreign policy than in helping fellow beings who were in desperate need of help."

Eventually, however, the Johnson administration relented and joined Canada and Australia in sending shiploads of gift wheat to India that year and the next. Port facilities and transport were unable to move the mountains of grain to stricken areas fast enough. Hundreds of thousands died of starvation, but for almost two years an estimated 60 million Indians were kept alive largely by American food shipments.

Some American taxpayers, then and later, resented being asked to bear the burden of feeding countries like India, which were not making all-out efforts to increase food production or reduce population. Their views were reflected in a letter to *Ms.* magazine by D. Ruth Bussey of New Mexico:

"I am tired of being told that I must cut my food consumption because of 'the poor starving ———' (fill in the blank with your favorite nation). India, for example, has more cattle than any other nation in the world. However, the killing or eating of cattle is prohibited by religious laws in India. According to my calculations, India's cattle could consume almost enough food to feed the total human population of India. I am sorry that children (and adults) are starving, but I don't want my children to join them. In short, I do not feel that the United States can feed the world."

The United States began changing its emphasis from offering direct food aid to helping poor countries increase their own food production through its Agency for International Development (AID). Norman Borlaug warned the Indian minister of food and agriculture, C. V. Subrimaniam, that he must triple expenditures on fertilizer, irrigation, and farm credit, and give full support to India's Mexican-trained agronomists. Annoyed, Subrimaniam sought to talk him down.

"I will not be silenced, Mr. Minister!" Borlaug shouted in exasperation. " . . . I could not go to sleep with my conscience if I did not say these things to you. . . . You have got to give them . . . fertilizers and credit! If you don't do those things, then I tell you that you and your government are sitting on a volcano."

In a broadcast in April 1966, Prime Minister Indira Gandhi expressed her government's determination to solve the food problem, declaring, "The current drought has a lesson for us. It is absolutely imperative that agricultural productivity is improved to a point where . . . we have a reasonable margin of safety. We simply cannot afford another gamble in rains."

India doubled appropriations for agricultural development. Heavy purchases of imported fertilizer began replenishing the soil, which had lost much of its nutrients after thousands of years of farming. The demand for fertilizer was so intense in Indian villages that when the supply ran out at one local warehouse, frustrated farmers in the line rioted.

There was also turbulence at Tanjore when district land-owners began planting Borlaug's new semi-dwarf wheat seeds in 1968. Half the farm workers struck for higher wages and a share of the bigger harvest the new seeds would bring. In bloody battles between strikers and nonstrikers, forty-two farm workers were killed.

The new seeds were eagerly sought by black marketeers. So many thieves stole them from research stations and experimental plots that armed troops had to be posted as guards. One black market gang nevertheless overpowered guards at a university research station and held knives to their throats while the semi-dwarf plots were raided. Unfortunately for customers of the black marketeers, the stolen experimental strains proved infertile.

The 1968 harvest ran fully 35 per cent larger than the previous year's. After local granaries were filled, there was no place left to store the mountains of surplus wheat. School had to be dismissed in many villages because schoolhouses were the only other uninhabited buildings capable of storing the grain. Even then much of it had to be heaped in the open until boxcars could be obtained to take it to New Delhi. Fortunately the rains were late and the wheat got away in time. The jubilant Indian government issued a special postage stamp to celebrate its wheat revolution.

By 1972, thanks to Borlaug's semi-dwarf wheat seeds, India was able to grow more than 26 million tons of wheat, the third largest crop in the world. It seemed as though hunger, the age-old scourge of India, had at last been conquered by modern agricultural science, which was now providing food for an additional 70 million Indians.

But then the country once more fell on lean years. The worst famine in three decades threatened a fourth of India's 580 million people as drought in some states, flood in others, ruined crops and destroyed cattle. In the rest of India the Green Revolution was crippled by skyrocketing prices for oil. Despite drastic cuts in the use of oil-based fertilizer and fuel for irrigation pumps, India was forced to spend half its meager foreign exchange for oil imports. Some farmers withheld scarce crops to sell them at inflated prices. Starvation once more ravaged India.

"It is, of course, a set official policy not to admit the starvation deaths," commented the *Indian Express.* "But that cannot hide the ugly reality."

Newsweek's Indian correspondent reported in June 1973, "Human greed and corruption have kept food and water from a number of the neediest areas. What's more, the myopic pride of some of the governments involved, which refuse even to acknowledge the potential catastrophe, has delayed imports of relief supplies so long that they may not be distributed in time." One official in India's Foreign Ministry told journalists not to visit these areas because "we are sick and tired of these horror stories about India."

Desperate mobs began to riot, looting grain shops in Agra, smashing cars of the rich in Bombay, plundering a government warehouse in Limdi. In Tumsar they attacked the home of a politician and seized his hoarded tons of rice and cattle feed. When a policeman tried to stop them, they stoned him to death and dragged his body through the streets.

The United States donated $67 million worth of food to India in 1973. But the famine only worsened in 1974, when a West Bengal farmer told newsmen, "We have had no food for ten days. Now, even the leaves and the wild roots are becoming scarce."

American opinion was outraged that year when the Indian government exploded an atomic bomb. "They spent a lot of money on that bomb that should have been spent on something productive instead of something provocative," angrily declared Congressman W. R. Poage, chairman of the House Agriculture Committee.

Washington nevertheless offered India a sizable contribu-

Bengali children. (FAO)

tion of low-cost food under Public Law 480, the Food for Peace program. But Prime Minister Indira Gandhi, stung by American criticism and resenting Indian dependence on the United States, bought 2 million tons of rice on the open market and began negotiating with the Soviet Union. She was disappointed in 1975 when an India-Soviet trade agreement failed to provide wheat, fertilizer, and oil products in the large quantities India urgently needed.

Part of India's food problem is the faulty storage of grain on farms. According to the UN Development Program, 10 million tons—twice the amount India imported in 1974—are spoiled each year by rats, birds, insects, and rain. FAO and Indian experts are seeking to replace the traditional jute sacks and mud containers used by farmers to store grain at home with cheap pest- and moisture-proof bins.

But even if food spoilage can be prevented and the Green

Revolution revived, it is doubtful if India could ever raise enough food to feed its swelling population. Even at the height of India's bumper crops, the U.S. Department of Agriculture observed: "Distributing present food supplies in India as far as they could go at the rate of 2,300 calories per person per day (minimum adequate level) would mean that a tenth of that country's 580 million people would have nothing at all to eat. If this food were distributed at the U.S. consumption rate (3,190 calories per person per day), 153 million Indians would starve."

Not only has India failed to curtail its production of human beings, but its citizens also live longer because of better medical care. Average life expectancy in India was only twenty-three years after World War II; today it is forty-eight years, requiring twice as much food. Even if India is able to double its wheat and rice production by the year 2000, the population will also have doubled, to a staggering 1,200,000,000 people.

"India will cope with these problems if it can slow down the growth of population," said Norman Borlaug. "If it does reduce the birth rate . . . India can feed itself—but only if there is political stability. The danger is that hunger will disrupt the stability. Anger builds into frustration, and a hungry man is not rational. There comes a time in his misery when he will kill for food—if not for himself, then for his family."

As Mahatma Gandhi once observed, "To the millions who have to go without two meals a day, the only acceptable form in which God dare appear is food."

8

Hunger
in Asia

When Borlaug went to Pakistan in 1963 to see how his
Mexican semi-dwarf wheats were thriving in Asia, he found
the experimental plants limp and drooping.

"What the hell is *this?*" he exploded. "You haven't fed
these damn things. They haven't been properly fertilized!"

An administrator of the Pakistani research institute explained that a top official had strictly limited the amount of
fertilizer that could be used for each experimental plot.
Borlaug went to bed fuming at bureaucrats. He was awak-
ened at dawn by two young Mexican-trained Pakistani
agronomists who put their fingers to their lips and indicated
that he should dress. Then they led him to a secluded plot.

"The sun was not yet up," he recalled, "but there was light
enough for me to see that small green patch. There they
were—the dwarfs—thrusting up their heavy heads of grain
. . . happy and vigorous, and as beautiful as I had ever seen
them growing in the Yaquí. Unknown to those stuffy officials, these two courageous young scientists had sown a

second generation from their samples and had fed them the correct amount of fertilizer. The plants looked beautiful. . . . They called them by another name, a name not even hinting that they were of Mexican origin! I could have danced! We shook hands; we laughed together. I took a closer look at that little green patch and knew in a moment we had something on our hands for Pakistan—and for India."

But as events soon proved, "miracle" seeds well-fertilized were not enough. Asians who could barely survive when crop-growing weather was favorable were plunged into catastrophe when their regions were swept by drought or floods.

In August 1974 the waters of the Brahmaputra River in northern Bangladesh, swollen by monsoon rains and melting Himalayan snows, began rising rapidly. Farm laborer Abdul Jabber and his three sons worked desperately with other villagers to protect their lands.

A cry of alarm went up as the surging waters tore through the embankment built to hold them. The whole region was quickly deluged by raging floods. Some families were swept away and drowned. Abdul Jabber and his family fled to safety on higher ground. He now had no way of feeding them. The summer rice crop had been washed away, wiping out jobs—and food—for everyone.

Panic and chaos followed the disastrous flooding of the Brahmaputra. Along with thousands of other families, the Jabbers sought shelter in a railway station, from which they were eventually evacuated to a refugee tent camp in Rangpur. Here 5,000 people were kept alive on relief rations of wheat flour. There were soon 4,500 such camps with an estimated 15 million people sharing the plight of the Jabber family, at least half of them children.

World relief shipments were late in arriving. In two weeks more than 100,000 people starved to death. For political

Refugees in Bangladesh. (UNICEF)

reasons, food minister Abdul Momen tried to dismiss reports of widespread famine as "exaggerated." When police came upon starving people in the streets, they herded them into the relief camps and kept them there under guard so that they would not stir up national unrest.

Bangladesh has no dairy herds; none of its preschool children get any milk. If all the milk powder the government was able to import were equally distributed among them, there would be only enough for one glass of milk per child for the entire year. A diet consisting largely of rice alone—and little of that during the floods—left the malnourished children vulnerable to epidemics sweeping the camps.

"I thought it was the end of the world for Bangladesh," declared UNICEF field coordinator Anowar Hussain when he inspected another refugee camp in Kurigram in October.

"Bodies were just lying around—mostly women and children—and I could see ribs sticking through them. Most were dead."

Lord Ritchie Calder observed that countries like Bangladesh ranked low on the list of those helped by food-donor countries. First priority was given to countries where food aid could help people get back to work and become self-sufficient in agriculture. The consequence of this policy, Ritchie Calder noted, was that "whole populations are marked for extermination as a matter of calculated judgment. The people of Bangladesh are a write-off."

In contrast, Taiwan has been successful in feeding its 12 million people largely because of an extensive and expensive agricultural aid program initiated by the United States for political reasons. To bolster Chiang Kai-shek after his fall in China, a U.S.-Chinese Joint Commission on Rural Reconstruction was set up in Taiwan. With the aid of American technology, money, and materials, agricultural production for this area was increased at the steady rate of 5.5 per cent a year.

Washington was less interested in helping Indonesia, where more than half the people live on only 1,500 calories a day. Nine out of ten Indonesians earn less than $1 a week, and some less than 1¢ a week. One major reason: There are 40 million more of them now than there were in 1966, when General Suharto overthrew President Sukarno.

War in Indochina brought hunger to an area that once grew enough rice for export. The use of napalm by American bombers to defoliate fields in which Communist soldiers might be concealed left millions of acres of fertile land scarred and lost to food production. Millions of farmers also fled their fields when they were turned into battlegrounds.

New York Times correspondent Sydney Schanberg, the last American newsman in Cambodia before it fell to the Khmer Rouge, declared that he felt tormented by the malnourished and starving children left by the war there. "In those faces," he declared, "I can see the faces of my daughters."

In Vietnam, during the last stages of the fighting, Buddhist nuns improvised country orphanages to feed thousands of orphaned or abandoned youngsters. "For us the main thing is to keep alive the children on the danger list," said one nun, "and to prevent as many deaths from malnutrition as possible." She explained how Buddhists who helped them managed to provide some food for the orphanages: "They buy feed rice, broken grain mixed with straw which is usually fed to hogs. They add a little Nhoc Mam (pickled fish) to it and pray patiently that time will pass and bring them wisdom of the Buddha. What else can they do?"

Hunger is no stranger to Afghanistan, where more than a million people either scratch a bare living on 6,000-to-10,000-foot mountains or drive herds through snow-covered passes. In the drought of 1970–72 about 100,000 people, including 40,000 under age twelve, began starving. Slaughtering their beasts of burden for food, they also ate their seed grains and local grasses. Forced to sell all their household goods and every stitch of spare clothing, they were reduced to destitution.

In some villages a third of the people perished. UNICEF mounted a crash relief effort called Operation Tez ("Help"). A special team, including three volunteers recruited from tourists, distributed high-protein U.S. AID corn-soy milk (CSM) to children in the affected mountain areas.

The team worked twelve hours a day trying to reach as many children as possible swiftly. People traveled fifteen miles on foot to get to food rendezvous points. "Many children were weak, in rags and eating grass," reported Brigadier A. N. M. Nambiar. Volunteer Robert Bayliss reported from one food station, "We can only feed 200 children, and there are many we have to turn away even though their need is equally great."

Many Afghanistanis who had sold their land to keep from

starving moved their families into caves. "In all of them there were young children who seemed to be on their last legs," related UNICEF officer John Balcomb, "some too weak to utter more than a feeble cry." One man sadly held up his two-year-old daughter—the last survivor of his five children.

In the region's schools Balcomb found children aged six to twelve numb with hunger: "Some were like wizened old men, their skin tight over their cheekbones, their eyes staring dully." These were the children with strength enough to attend school; half as many again had stayed home, too weak to walk. Brigadier Nambiar arranged with the teachers to handle new food shipments expected from UNICEF.

"We will bring it to all the schools we can reach by jeep,"

Afghanistani mother and child. (UNICEF/JOHN BALCOMB)

he explained. "We are depending on you, the teachers, to distribute it impartially to all the children—enough to last each child through the winter and enough for him to take home to tide his little brothers and sisters over the winter, too. We are putting our trust in you because you are members of an honorable profession which holds the future of Afghanistan in your hands."

How many children's lives were saved by Operation Tez, and how many were lost, was never learned. Communications between the government and the remote mountain regions, as in many countries of Asia, were barely marginal.

The UN's World Health Organization estimates that at least 70 million Asians are affected by malnutrition year in, year out, some 6 million severely. Up to 40 per cent of all pregnant Asian women suffer from nutritional anemia. Not surprisingly, many Asian nations have begun looking to China for answers to the problem of hunger.

For centuries drought, floods, and worn-out lands had brought death and misery to the Chinese people. Against insuperable odds and with the largest population in the world to feed, the People's Republic of China had managed to provide enough food for all for the first time in the country's history.

Before the Chinese Communists took power in 1949, peasants had feared China's soldiers as human locusts. Marching from village to village, the troops ate up stores of grain, killing villagers who protested. Significantly, the Chinese word for peace, *ho-ping,* means literally "food for all."

The Chinese have always understood the importance of food in conditioning human behavior. "It is difficult to tell the difference between right and wrong," went an old Chinese proverb, "when the stomach is empty." The traditional Chinese greeting was not "Good day," or "How are you?" but simply "Have you eaten?"

Centuries of constant natural disasters made survival in

China a matter of luck. In the province of Canton, 80 per cent of the land used to be subject to drought, the other 20 per cent to flooding. A Cantonese saying went, "Three days of drought stops the waterwheel; one day of rain begins a flood." To survive, the Chinese were often forced to borrow heavily at usurious rates from the landlords, that 4 per cent of the population who owned 69 per cent of the land. In the famine of 1927–29, affecting six provinces, up to 75 per cent of the population in some regions starved to death.

An inkling of what life was like in those years was given to visiting actress Shirley MacLaine by a Chinese girl whose peasant grandfather, lacking food for his family, had pleaded with his brother in Chiang Kai-shek's army for a loan of enough grain to let them survive the winter. When his brother refused, the girl's grandfather took some of the grain. The brother had him arrested and executed.

"We live on wild herbs which we collected on the mountain ridge," the girl recalled, adding, "I couldn't walk well . . . because my bones had no calcium. Sometimes we had millet but when I saw my image in the bowl I knew it was only water. . . . I was always miserable, always cold, and always hungry. I never laughed and became very sullen."

Under the corrupt rule first of warlords, then of Chiang's Kuomintang, ancient systems of dikes and irrigation works fell into total disrepair. These rulers also failed to provide relief or assistance during famines, letting rich landowners take advantage of calamity by buying out desperate small farmers for a few coins. The rich were allowed to profiteer further by hoarding grain during famines.

The average life expectancy in China during the 1920's was only twenty-eight years. Living on the edge of starvation, the Chinese had such low resistance to disease that epidemics carried off hundreds of thousands every year. Babies had to be breast-fed for up to four years because no other food was available.

American correspondent Edgar Snow watched masses of Chinese starve to death in Suiyuan in 1929. In *Red Star over China* he wrote: "Have you ever seen a man—a good honest man who has worked hard, a 'law-abiding citizen,' doing no serious harm to anyone—when he has had no food for more than a month? It is a most agonizing sight. His dying flesh hangs from him in wrinkled folds; you can clearly see every bone in his body; his eyes stare out unseeing; and even if he is a youth of twenty he moves like an ancient crone, dragging himself from spot to spot. . . . Children are even more pitiable, with their little skeletons bent over and misshapen, their crooked bones, their little arms like twigs, and their purpling bellies, filled with bark and sawdust, protruding like tumors."

While the famine raged, the American-financed China International Famine Relief Commission sought to irrigate some of the lands baked by drought. Chiang Kai-shek's officials promptly bought up all the lands scheduled for irrigation for a few cents an acre.

More than one million Chinese died in the famine which overtook northern China in 1941–43. American correspondent Jack Belden reported: "Women exchanged their babies, saying, 'You eat mine, I'll eat yours.' When a man was going to die, he dug a pit and sat inside and asked neighbors to fill in the earth when he was dead. Afterward, however, no one could be found to fill in the pits, for all were either dead or too weak to shovel earth. Men sold their children first, then their wives."

The roads to the Taihang Mountains were filled with corpses, beside trees which had been stripped of every bud and all their bark. In some places people lived for a few days longer by eating the wastes of silkworms and some baked earth. Belden noted, "I was ashamed to go from one Kuomintang general to another, eating delicacies from their well-laid tables, while peasants were scraping the fields outside the *yamens* for roots and wild grass to stuff into their griping stomachs."

After centuries of such cruel neglect, the Chinese peasantry eagerly supported Mao Tse-tung's Red Army, whose soldiers never robbed villages of food but grew their own, and even helped peasants plant and reap their harvests. Soon after the Communists took power in 1949, Mao proclaimed more food for the Chinese people as a primary goal of his government.

But the huge problem of hunger in China was not quickly solved. In 1959–60 floods and drought destroyed almost half of the harvest. The failure of China's overambitious Great Leap Forward, collectivizing agriculture prematurely, aggravated the problem. Millions were forced to eat wild herbs, and 70,000 people reportedly died in Kansu province. Observers agreed, however, that the Communists had avoided even worse famine by efficient and scrupulously fair rationing.

"I arrived in Peking in the terrible winter of 1960–61," reported Swedish scholar Sven Lindqvist. " . . . The streets were filled with endless queues, waiting outside the communal feeding centers. The dream of having just one good square meal hung over the city like a mirage over the desert. . . . When the ration consists of rice or wheat flour, it is meagre, but enough to live on. For several years now it has been mixed with sweet potatoes, barley meal and other low-grade cereal flour. This means hunger and apathy."

Rations improved steadily as China was able to import Canadian and Australian wheat, and better Chinese harvests became available. By 1965 the Chinese had recovered to the extent of even accumulating reserves of grain and meat. In that year Edgar Snow had a discussion with Mao Tse-tung about American food production, informing Mao that only 8 per cent of the population was needed to produce more food than Americans could eat.

"Mao asked me to repeat the figure," Snow related. "When I did so he shook his head skeptically. How could that be? was all he said."

If China cannot hope to compete with the United States in food production, it has nevertheless done an outstanding job by Asian standards. Now, even in the hardest years, everyone eats—a far cry from the terrible epochs when famine carried off millions of Chinese at a time.

"The people of China," noted the Committee of Concerned Asian Scholars, "say they have done in twenty years what two thousand years of emperors and feudal landlords could not accomplish." No longer must any Chinese beg in the streets or at landlords' houses for food.

Peasant families now not only share communal harvests, but also own small private plots on which they grow vegetables for their own use. When the Communists took power, only 5 per cent of Chinese land was irrigated. Today—95 per cent.

Reporting from Linhsien in 1974, *New York Times* correspondent Harrison Salisbury observed: "This was an arid and barren countryside that traditionally had . . . drought nine years out of ten, and poor peasants traditionally sold their children, and went out to beg to earn enough to escape starvation. . . . Since the construction of an enormous canal . . . life has changed amazingly." Bumper crops have led to a healthy people "who suffer no undernourishment, and no serious dietary diseases."

Life expectancy for the average Chinese has been raised to more than fifty years, highest in the nation's history.

Sartaj Aziz, director of FAO's Commodities and Trade Division, studied China's collective agriculture intensively during several visits. He concluded that it "represents the most remarkable and ingenious endeavor for what we usually call integrated rural development." The Chinese were notably well off by Asian standards, and this well-being was evenly distributed, with the basic needs of food, clothing, shelter, education, and medicine met for every Chinese.

"How many other countries of Asia, Africa, and Latin America can make this claim," Aziz asked, "even for the forseeable future? . . . What can these countries learn from China?"

Noting that the Chinese were able to mobilize the unemployed and underemployed in improving the land, building dikes, dams, and irrigation channels, and constructing roads, he pointed out, "In most other less developed countries of Asia, available manpower cannot be utilized fully, at least partly because of the pattern of land ownership."

The FAO must be carefully nonpartisan and nonpolitical in its work of seeking to alleviate world hunger. But Norman R. Michie, FAO information liaison officer, declared: "Certainly China has made remarkable progress in solving its food problem. The FAO would have no hesitation in recommending to underdeveloped nations that they investigate the methods by which China has managed to lift itself up by its bootstraps and provide sufficient food for its enormous population."

Asian famine caused by drought and floods is recognized by the world as an emergency, but simple hunger is not.

"Many Americans are under the delusion that an Asian can live happily 'on a bowl of rice a day,'" observed Dr. Paul R. Ehrlich. "Such a diet means slow starvation for an Asian, just as it would for an American. . . . The Population Crisis Committee estimates that three and one-half million people will starve to death this year, mostly children."

The future of an Asia with 4 billion people to feed by the year 2000 is not one that is cheerful to contemplate.

9
Hunger
in Africa

In Mali a herdsman who lost his cattle to drought led his family on a grueling 200-mile trek to the nearest refugee camp. When they finally staggered into the camp, they found that emergency rations had been largely exhausted by crowds of refugees already there. A relief worker managed to supply them with four minimal, children's portions of gruel.

There were five children in the family.

"My wife and I will go without," the man said impassively. Then his voice broke. "But how can I decide which of my five children shall starve?"

Ironically, the starving children who found food in West Africa's refugee camps were not always the lucky ones. Many whose systems could not handle sudden gorging literally ate themselves to death.

The terrible drought in the Sahel, affecting Mali, Mauritania, Senegal, Upper Volta, Niger, and Chad, began in 1968. "The heat is so stifling in these summer months," observed UNICEF official Leon Davico, "that you are tempted to offer an empire for a square inch of grass and shade." Trees were dying everywhere. The parched landscape, once fertile valleys and fields of millet, resembled the surface of the moon. Decaying carcasses lay strewn where once herds had grazed.

Children surviving the drought were often little more than skin-covered bones, bent over by malnutrition, too feeble to stand, let alone walk or crawl. Debilitated and dehydrated, many died from ailments like diarrhea, pneumonia, and bronchitis. An outbreak of measles in Agadez, Niger, killed hundreds, and cholera carried off many in Upper Volta.

Not until September 1972 did African governments of the Sahel report the emergency to the FAO. "They knew they could not prevent drought," observed an American diplomat in Africa, "but they did not want to admit that they had no way of helping their people." The FAO and the six governments declared the Sahel a disaster area and sent a mission which worked seven days a week, eighteen hours a day, distributing 450,000 tons of grain.

When the crisis grew worse in November 1973, the UN and FAO issued a joint appeal to the nations of the world for more food and funds. But an international relief effort became bogged down in local mismanagement and corruption.

More than 200,000 tons of grain piled up at African ports awaiting distribution. Spoiling in the open, it was also easy prey to thieves, locusts, wharf rats, and quelea quelea birds, which can consume twice their considerable weight daily. Relief officials pleaded in vain with railroad workers and truckers to move the food to where it was needed before the badly delayed rainy season began.

"If the nomads are hungry," said one Chad colonel indifferently, "let them come to population centers."

The FAO found food bound for Chad stalled at the Nigerian-Chad border because the wife of Chad's president owned the national truck monopoly. She insisted that the food must be carried into Chad on her own trucks, at twice the

This nomad family walked nearly seventy-five miles in search of food. (FAO/B. IMEVBORE)

normal rate for freight, even though every hour's delay meant greater suffering for her own people. In Ethiopia truckers refused to transport food because other cargos paid higher rates.

Instead of distributing relief grain, some Mali officials sold it to local merchants, who then resold it to their starving countrymen at an enormous profit. An equitable distribution of food aid failed even when some of the Western nations sought to bypass the ports by flying it in to the hungry.

"When the plane flies overhead they rush to the airfield," reported Peace Corps worker Nancy Necker in Agadez, Niger, "hoping to get the food before it is sent to the distribution centers. Some of the people have been badly trampled by others trying to get to the food sacks." Belgian air force pilot Marcel Vleugels reported, "The food vanishes almost as it hits the ground." A Niger tribesman told a U.S.

correspondent, "If the food from the sky stops, we are gone, we are dead."

That did not keep African merchants of airplane fuel from jumping their prices 500 per cent to planes bringing in aid.

When torrential rains finally pelted Africa south of the Sahara, ending a six-year drought, floods further hampered food relief. Floodwaters washed out roads, isolating communities except for foot and camel caravans. Thousands of tons of food continued to spoil in the coastal ports.

It will be a long time before the people of the Sahel recover from their disaster. "It will affect the children in the area even four or five years from now," predicted Dr. Ibrahima Konate, executive director for Sahel relief. "Maybe our countries will find that they have unusual numbers of handicapped people." The average life span in the Sahel is now estimated at only thirty-eight years.

The ability of the Sahel economy itself to recover is in serious question. Its once-fertile fields have been reclaimed by the desert, and its once-vast herds have been almost wiped out. "It will take twenty to thirty years to get the herds back up," mourned one Mali official.

Agricultural experts blamed the drought in the Sahelian nations on the unwitting rape of the land by its own people. Herdsmen had overgrazed the savanna with cattle, goats, sheep, donkeys, and camels, and had cut down trees and shrubs as animal feed. Almost all vegetation had also been removed as fuel for cooking and home heating.

The stripping of millions of acres of savanna had brought about the first great alteration in the world's climate in almost 300 years, according to H. H. Lamb, director of the Climatic Research Unit of the University of East Anglia in England. It had caused a severe six-year decline in rainfall, permitting the Sahara to spread southward at the rate of thirty miles a year, because vegetation is essential to the rain cycle.

"We have eaten more sand this year than in our thirteen

years here," declared a European missionary in western Niger in 1974. "There is not enough vegetation to hold back the desert." The immensity of the tragedy was not fully understood by the Sahelian governments themselves until the herds began dying in great numbers, and millions of tribesmen sought new grazing lands in the south.

Nomads poured into the Ivory Coast and Ghana, letting their starving animals poach on the croplands of subsistence farmers. This invasion brought bloody battles between outraged farmers and desperate herdsmen.

Many economic experts believe that the West African nations must either change or perish. Millions of herdsmen will have to give up the nomadic life for farming. The transition will not be easy. An attempt to bring it about failed in Mauritania. Herdsmen, one government official concluded, lack the "gardening mentality." In Niger a Tuareg chief's son agreed. "We would rather die," he vowed, "than leave the desert."

Can the parched grazing and crop lands of the Sahel be

Farmers in Dahomey. (FAO/C. BAVAGNOLI)

restored to feed its people? Drought can be fought by new water resources, available for tapping under areas of desert, located by infrared satellite photos made by the American Skylab crew in orbit around the earth. Dr. Edward Fei, AID's regional coordinator for Africa, thinks irrigation and proper conservation measures could make the Sahel self-sufficient, at a cost of $10 billion over twenty-five years.

Bruno van de Walle, a UN official in Agadez, is less optimistic. "By the time a drought reaches such proportions ... it is too late," he wrote. "The land and the people have lost too much to recover."

Niger's ambassador to the United States, Abdoulaye Diallo, urged Washington to institute a program of cloud-seeding to make rain for his country. But many African governments are suspicious of any plans the West might propose. "What we are afraid of," admitted Senegal's planning minister, Ousmae Seck, "is that some of the developed countries will impose priorities on us that only benefit *their* economies."

When agricultural reporter Charles Morrow Wilson visited a Firestone rubber plantation in Libera after World War II, natives were eating roots to survive. A young planter told Wilson, "The best they ever had is a once-a-day afternoon meal." He went on to say that when he had first arrived in Liberia, he had sought to feed the workers a breakfast of imported canned dog food. His employer had bawled him out for feeding such "expensive" food to rubber tappers.

One of Africa's most terrible famines was caused not by drought, abuse of the land, or colonial mistreatment, but by tribal warfare. In 1966 the Ibo tribe of Nigeria revolted against the government, declaring their homeland of Biafra independent. The Nigerian government threw up a sea blockade, cutting off the Biafrans from their traditional diet of protein-rich fish, and also from the supplemental food they imported.

Hunger turned to starvation for millions of Biafrans during two and a half years of civil war. News photographers made the reality of famine vivid for a shocked world.

From a refugee camp in western Biafra, Father Sean Guina reported, "I was going around the wards one day recently when I noticed four children lying on a bed. One of them was dead, but I couldn't distinguish him at first from the others. On another bed, an infant was sucking its mother's breast. The mother was dead."

Relief shipments for the Biafrans were slow in coming because Nigeria's raw materials were important to many Western countries, which hesitated to offend the government.

"We have no intention," declared President Lyndon B. Johnson, " of interfering in Nigerian affairs."

The Nigerian government insisted that all food and medicine for the Biafrans must be funneled through its hands. Biafrans refused to accept any relief donated in this way for fear that the Nigerians would poison it. Meanwhile millions of Biafran babies were dying of hunger.

"Even if the war stopped tomorrow," warned Sister Mary Lorcan, an Irish nun working in the refugee camps, "hundreds of thousands would die. There's no saving them." She added in despair, "I just can't understand the world!"

The International Red Cross described starvation in Biafra as "one of the great disasters of human experience."

One relief worker angrily told an American correspondent, "To hell with whatever side you're on! There are thousands of people dying in that bit of Africa. If we don't get some food in there, there won't be any Biafrans left!"

News stories finally aroused public opinion. Many countries, including the United States, began flying in food and medicine, often risking being shot down. In fact, the Nigerians did shoot down a Red Cross relief plane.

But by November 1968 some 300,000 Biafrans had already died of malnutrition. And when the civil war finally ended

Woman gathering buds in Upper Volta. (UNICEF/BERNARD PIERRE WOLFF)

with Nigeria's victory in January 1970, it had cost 2 million lives—most of them Biafran civilians who had starved to death. As in the Sahel tragedy, which was already underway, too little food had come too late.

In many regions of Africa hunger is a normal condition. The UN World Health Organization estimates that 19 million African children suffer from malnutrition, 3 million of them severely. Rickets are prevalent among North African infants and children. Iron deficiency is suffered by up to 50 per cent of all African women.

Inspecting conditions in Dar es Salaam, Tanzania, a doctor named Lema reported that 30 per cent of the children under five were malnourished. He found seven out of ten of those youngsters hospitalized with severe kwashiorkor. "Open sores spread over the flesh, particularly on the thighs and lower body," Dr. Lema reported, "so that the child looks as if he had been badly burned."

To the west of Dar es Salaam, the death rate for children under the age of five was 50 per cent.

In Upper Volta the soil is so poor and rains so unreliable that no source of food, however meager, is neglected in the incessant struggle to get enough to eat. Women gather buds of a blossoming tree to make into food, drink, and animal feed. Possibly the poorest country in the world today, Upper Volta has only one doctor for every 70,000 inhabitants, who have a life expectancy of only thirty-two years.

Most of Ethiopia's people live in fertile, well-watered highlands. But the unchecked birth rate has produced a shortage of farmland, compelling many to migrate to lower altitudes to attempt to cultivate drier, eroded acreage.

"Farmers simply ploughed, sowed their seed, and hoped for the best," reported UNICEF official John Balcomb. "Little or nothing was done to improve yields through better seeds, fertilizers, or minor irrigation. Most were tenants and had no real incentive to initiate better agricultural practices: if they got a better than average crop, their rent was raised—also their taxes. This was the situation when the drought hit, and it was because of it that the effects of the drought were so devastating."

The profound discontent of Ethiopia's hungry farmers was one of the reasons Emperor Haile Selassie was toppled from a throne that traced as far back as King Solomon.

Kenya is one of the bright spots of Africa. Thanks to the Green Revolution, hybrid strains of corn and wheat have increased yields from an average of thirteen to seventy-one bushels an acre. Some 300,000 acres, two-thirds of all small farms, were planted with the new high-yield corn seeds. Almost overnight Kenya became a corn-exporting nation.

In the Ivory Coast, too, new high-yield rice has been able to buy time in the race against an exploding birth rate by doubling the size of harvests.

Overpopulation rather than drought is the cause of much hunger in North Africa. In Egypt pellagra, caused by vitamin deficiency, attacks 400,000 people a year. Despite President Anwar el-Sadat's reopening of the Suez Canal and attempts to attract large-scale foreign investments, nutrition is likely to become an even more severe problem in Egypt because the already swollen population is expected to double again in just fifteen years.

Poverty and undernourishment are also the rule in Tunisia, but like most Muslims the people often share what little they have with the hungry. "If anyone needs bread or flour he is sure to find someone who will give it to him," said one village wife. "He has only to ask." A Tunisian elder explained, "We owe God obedience, and he owes us our daily bread."

Once it was thought that freedom from colonial oppression would solve all of Africa's problems. But despite the achievement of independence by one country after another, the people have found that politics has been unable to stem hunger in the face of drought, eroded farmland, primitive agriculture, poor transport, and overpopulation.

Africans nevertheless continue to hope for miracles. Many fail to recognize that planned parenthood, voluntarily reducing the number of mouths to be fed, is a necessary adjunct to reducing malnutrition and starvation. Instead they prefer to believe that they need to increase their numbers to prosper.

More realistic are the Shona tribes of Rhodesia who sing as they work in their fields:

> This year do not throw away the chaff,
> Save your poorest food,
> For the famine is coming.

10

Hunger in Latin America

An American woman teacher visiting an Indian mountain region of Peru wondered where all the children she saw got their chewing gum. The local priest corrected her: "It is not gum, *señora*. They are chewing coca leaves."

"Are coca leaves a source of food?"

"No, a source of cocaine."

"Cocaine!"

"They chew it to deaden the pains of hunger, *señora*," the priest explained. "They are always hungry. They always will be. Our population doubles every twenty-three years. Where can poor Peru get all the food to feed so many?"

Many rural Peruvians, lacking land, work, and food, move to Lima. Living in caves and bamboo or tin shacks in hillside communities known as *barriadas,* they search for any kind of work in the city. Their children go to school, where at least they get free hot lunches made possible by AID.

Richard Apodoca, U.S. AID officer in Peru, explained what the hot-lunch program meant to more than 300,000

Peruvian school children: "A lot of them walk to school, a distance of anywhere from two to four miles. If it weren't for that hot lunch, they'd be too weak to get much out of their studies. Ministry of Education records show that in schools where they serve the lunch, enrollment has increased by as much as 35 per cent. What's more, if it weren't for that food, a lot of parents would have to let their children go to work."

Until 1969, when a left-wing military junta took power, most Peruvians lived in virtual slavery. Less than one per cent of the population owned 76 per cent of the country's agricultural lands. Mariano Quispe, a Peruvian peasant in the Valley of the Incas near Cuzco, told a representative of FAO what life had been like for him and his family.

As a child worker on a hacienda, he had labored from early dawn to dusk for less than a penny a day. When he grew up, married, and had children, he earned 10¢ a day. "There were more mouths to feed," he related, "extreme poverty and insufficient clothing: our sons nearly died of cold and hunger. In fact, we lost one child soon after birth."

When Quispe and other peasants had tried to protest their exploitation, they had been beaten by overseers. "There were haciendas with their own dungeons," he recalled, "and the police who always defended the masters; they came on horseback, destroyed everything, flogged us, and if we protested, they took us away. . . . If we put up any resistance, they shot us; nobody cared if a peasant died. . . . My wife died as a result of the beating they gave her once when she was trying to prevent them from taking me away."

Pressed for more details of what his life had been like, Quispe replied, "All I remember is that I have always been hungry and cold, and I have tried to protect my family from hunger and cold. My life has been one enormous struggle, as enormous as the rainbow that joins the heaven and earth. Of my poor wife, what can I say? We didn't even have the time to look into each other's eyes."

One of his brothers, Quispe related, had been enticed to work on a distant hacienda by the promise of higher pay. Finding that the wages had to be spent in the hacienda company store for overpriced food, his brother had been forced to ask for credit. "Then, because he could not manage to pay back his debt, he had to remain there years and years, without even being able to marry, as though he were in an enormous open-air prison." A laborer who attempted to escape was denounced by the police, "and the man was pursued like a wild beast and obliged to return."

Conditions have improved for the Quispes of Peru since the new revolutionary government passed an Agrarian Reform Law in June 1969. Expropriated land was distributed among 193,000 formerly landless families. A new General Law of Water transferred all water ownership to the state, assuring irrigation for small farmers. Despite adverse climatic conditions, land reforms more than doubled the growth rate of Peruvian agriculture. The food supply, however, is still painfully small compared to Peru's population growth.

But Quispe was satisfied. "Now my grandchildren have enough to eat," he declared, "they can be clothed and they can be sent to college, because what the earth produces is for our benefit and not for any master."

The election of the Marxist regime of Salvador Allende in Chile during the early 1970's was another example of the revolutionary currents running against centuries of hunger in Latin America. More social upheavals undoubtedly lie ahead. An estimated million Latin Americans die every year from starvation and malnutrition. Notre Dame sociologist Donald N. Barrett described one slum where "two or three children [are] dying per week because of the ravenous dogs."

At one time Latin American corn had accounted for almost three-quarters of the world supply. But 5 million hungry new mouths every year have gradually reduced that surplus until today Latin America is forced to import food.

If that birth rate continues, by the end of the century the continent may have to feed 800 million people, as many as China today.

To reach the 2,300 minimum calories a day the FAO prescribes to prevent malnutrition, Latin America now requires a 400 per cent increase in its food supply. Malnutrition and its related diseases kill from twenty to forty times as many children as in the United States and Western Europe, according to Professor Nevin S. Scrimshaw, head of the Department of Nutrition and Food Science at Massachusetts Institute of Technology.

"Poverty in South America reaches a pitch almost beyond the comprehension of the average North American," wrote John Gunther in his book *Inside South America.* "Literally millions of citizens exist desperately or numbly on the edge of starvation a few hours by jet from New York."

A shanty town crowds close to modern apartment buildings in Venezuela. (WIDE WORLD PHOTOS)

North American cartoonists often poke fun at the *mañana* attitude of Latin Americans, depicting them slumped over under sombreros in constant siestas. But doctors recognize that much of this apathy represents a lack of energy caused by malnutrition. Diets of corn and beans, or of just cornmeal tortillas, do not provide the body with needed proteins, minerals, and vitamins. Parasites intensify the energy loss. Hookworms can rob victims of as much as half a pint of blood a day, causing fatal anemia.

Peace Corps volunteer Moritz Thomsen, a forty-eight-year-old farmer who went to work in Ecuador, told Senator Ernest F. Hollings what hunger is like in Latin America:

"There was hardly anything to eat in the town and we were caught up in a monumental lethargy. The Italian priests who dominated the religious life of the town sent a fresh plump Brother out to take charge of the mission. . . . When he was recalled, he had lost about forty pounds. . . . It wasn't that the people didn't want to feed him, it was simply that there was nothing to share; and many of the people were filled with shame and humiliation when the Brother, vacant-eyed and ribs jutting, left the town.

"It was the bananas that saved my life. When it was possible to buy them, I could generally manage to move around, but it meant eating bananas all day. Trying to set an example, I was clearing land on a daily schedule, and it became a fascinating problem in internal combustion to stuff the bananas into myself and see how far I could go. Two bananas would fill me up for forty or fifty minutes of low-keyed work; one banana would get me down the hill. Sixteen bananas would see me through until noon if I didn't work too fast or if the hordes of [children] didn't shatter all my plans with their hungry cries as I passed the last house on the street.

"But being hungry wasn't simply losing my energy and reaching a moment about eleven o'clock in the morning when I ran out of energy and I had to sit down about five minutes to plan the next move. . . . It was also a growing mental depression, a gray fog of hopelessness that grew in my head each day; I could feel myself getting stupider. Things became incomprehensible and irritating to me.

"Afternoons I usually stayed in the house and either slept or would just sit on a stool staring out of a window at the ocean. [With a] caloric intake limited to a bare subsistence level, you can't work more than three or four hours a day. There is only so much energy in a dish of rice and a piece of fish. There are just so many miles to a gallon of bananas, not one more. . . .

"I began to be aware that in the town there was scarcely a moment when a baby's crying didn't fill the air. . . ."

Latin Americans are understandably cynical when *gringo* officials make eloquent speeches glorifying liberty above full stomachs. Addressing the Inter-American Press Association, State Department diplomat Spruille Braden once proclaimed, "We prefer hunger to loss of liberty. . . . Any form of suffering, even death itself, is preferable to losing liberty!"

Dr. Juan José Arévalo, former president of Guatemala, observed sarcastically, "The millionaires produce hunger in ton lots . . . but do not suffer from it, nor do they even know it. They have never seen it passing by. . . . Hunger does not ride up the elevators of the Waldorf Astoria."

Small farmers in Latin America who are lucky enough to own a little land are often its prisoners, like Vertugio Herrera of Honduras. All his life he vainly sought to scratch a living from farmland beside the Ulúa River, chocolate-brown from the soils it constantly ripped away. At least once a year Herrera's land was ravaged by the flooding Ulúa. He vowed that if ever he could harvest one good season's crops, he would pay off all his debts and move somewhere far away. Vertugio Herrera never succeeded. Like most of his neighbors, he merely died trying.

In the Dominican Republic people in the countryside eat regular meals only once or twice a week, seeking their nourishment in snacks of sugar cane, pieces of local white cheese, crackers, oranges, or hot sausages. Many babies die of marasmus combined with gastroenteritis. When a tent clinic was set up in the town of Higüey, a horde of Dominican women descended upon it and almost tore the tent down to get flour and powdered milk for their children.

In Haiti a large population attempting to live off a badly eroded land suffers from severe malnutrition and kwashiorkor. Starvation threatened several hundred thousand Haitians in the summer of 1975 when drought killed the crops and only minimal relief aid arrived. Many who ate weeds to try to stay alive were poisoned.

In Colombia, villagers multiply so rapidly that the tiny rooms of flimsy shacks are crammed with large hungry families. What little food there is goes to the farmers so that they can work in the cane fields and sugar mills.

"Undernourishment means early death for many of the children," Dr. Alfredo Aguirre reported to the Population Council, "and if death fails to intervene . . . [they will suffer] delay in walking, retardation in speech development."

Colombian mothers have to spend 80 per cent of the family income on food to keep their broods alive. "Children between six months and four years of age are often allowed to die when attacked by any disease," Dr. Aguirre wrote, adding, "We have even seen mothers who objected to their children being treated and [who] were upset when curative measures were successful."

More than 100 infants die of malnutrition in Colombia every day, Arthur Hopcraft stated in his book, *Born to Hunger*. Despite this "death control," Colombia continues to double its population every twenty-two years. Poverty begets more children, declared Colombian president Alfonso López Michelson, and more children beget more poverty.

Most children born to the poor are doomed to crippled

om the hour of birth. Dr. J. M. Bengoa, chief of
nutrition unit, cited as typical a South American
who, by the age of two, had already had six eye
infections, ten lung infections, four attacks of bronchitis, and
five of diarrhea, measles, bronchopneumonia, and stomatitis.

"In twenty-four months," Dr. Bengoa, pointed out, "this
child has had nearly thirty attacks of illness and has had one
infection or another for about a third of his life. His diet has
been inadequate, with the result that each infection has led
to loss of weight from which he has never been able to
recover completely. At two years of age he is almost a year
behind in physical development."

A principal reason for hunger in Latin America is the lack
of agrarian reform. In a typical area of the Andes, large
haciendas use fertile valley land for grazing cattle, while the
peons are forced to cultivate tiny patches of corn and beans
in the poor soil of adjacent hillsides. Efforts by the United
States through the Alliance for Progress, stressing land
reform and self-help, have left the social structure of agrarian Latin America largely unchanged. The FAO presses for
land reform but progress is slow, because often the governments it deals with are controlled by the wealthy landowners.

In Brazil, Dom Helder Pessoa Câmara, archbishop of
Recife, was asked if he considered the Alliance the answer to
hunger in Latin America. "I did believe in it," he replied,
"but I don't any more. It cannot work, because the elite in
Latin America will not give up their privileges."

Northeast Brazil remains a hunger zone because military
rulers in that country refuse to abolish feudal systems of
land ownership, water rights, and food distribution. Most
people in this region receive only half the minimum daily
requirement of calories. A survey of their children showed
the average IQ to be only 75.

"In the northeast especially, millions live in subhuman

conditions," Dom Helder declared. "We must encourage them to rise to a human level. The oppressors keep their power by keeping the poor in servitude."

Brazil's military-industrial elite accused the archbishop of being "Fidel Castro in a cassock" and mounted terrorist attacks against a Catholic protest movement. Dom Helder was also regarded unfavorably by foreign governments with investments in Brazil when he pointed out that for every $1 million of investments, $4 million left the country in foreign profits. "For all the talk about 'foreign aid,'" he charged, "the rich are still getting richer, and the poor poorer, each day."

The greatest progress in Latin America has been achieved in Mexico, thanks to the Green Revolution. To appreciate how much things have changed, one has only to refer to John Reed's book *Insurgent Mexico,* published in 1914.

"At one of the houses I negotiated for dinner," Reed reported. "The woman spread out both her hands. 'We are all so poor now,' she said. 'A little water, some beans— *tortillas. . . .* It is all we eat in this house. . . . ' Milk? No. Eggs? No. Meat? No. Coffee? *Valgame Dios,* no!"

While Reed was cooking some tortillas and chili over a campfire, two peons in torn blankets turned up. Only after much urging could he get them to accept a few tortillas. "It was ludicrous and pitiful to see how wretchedly hungry they were," he noted, "and how they attempted to conceal it from us." Afterwards, one told Reed, "I have often wondered why the rich, having so much, want so much. The poor, who have nothing, want so very little. Just a few goats. . . . "

The Mexico of today has come a long way since that time of widespread hunger. Large estates have been expropriated, with 160 million acres now owned by small farmers. Major irrigation projects have increased production of wheat, cane sugar, tomatoes, fruit, corn, rice, cocoa, bananas, and wheat.

Volunteers in the Mexican rural works program make irrigation pipes. (FAO/F. BOTTS)

Although the fast-growing population is still a problem, Mexican life expectancy has been raised to sixty-eight years.

The Cuban government has also managed to end serious hunger among its people, even in the face of an economic boycott by the United States and the Organization of American States (OAS). In ten years Fidel Castro doubled Cuba's production of sugar, rice, citrus fruit, eggs, and vegetables. He also built up a Cuban herd of half a million dairy cattle. "In cattle raising we have given first priority to milk," he explained, "as this is the most complete food, one which is especially necessary for children, elderly people, the sick and others."

Castro rejected the arguments of advisers who wanted him to concentrate on raising beef cattle for export. He pointed out that many of the Third World countries were exporting meat to the developed countries—"the tragic colonial pattern of the starving feeding the well-fed." Cuba, he insisted, must help break that pattern, setting an example by using cattle to provide milk for its own people instead.

If there are sometimes food shortages, most Cubans credit Castro with at least seeing to it that available food is rationed fairly and equitably. One factory worker told visiting Jamaican playwright Barry Reckord, "People eat when the food's there . . . they can take it or leave it. Fidel left a life full of food to go hungry in the Sierra." Cubans know that for Castro efforts to provide nourishing food for everyone have a very high priority. "The over-all agricultural policy has been geared to the needs of the population," reports Dr. Eilif Liisberg, public health administrator of WHO's Division of Family Health, "so that the fisheries, the milk and meat production have been increased not for export but to improve the nutritional level of the population."

Nutritional disease, the scourge of Latin America, is not a problem in Cuba. Dr. Iraj Tabibzadeh, WHO medical officer,

As Cuban sugar production increased, new processing mills were built. (FAO/PRENSA LATINA)

observes that 50 per cent of the national budget is spent on health and education. Cuba is still a struggling country with many problems, but the people believe the government is doing an honest and conscientious job.

One hopeful development for Latin America is the experimentation by firms in the United States to develop new and more nutritious food substitutes. Swift and Company is working on a textured soybean food for Brazil. The Quaker Oats Company is selling a protein-enriched food in Guatemala and Colombia at a tenth of the cost of powdered milk. Called Incaperina, it is a vegetable mixture made of corn, soy-meal, and cottonseed meal. In El Salvador the Pillsbury Company is selling a fortified powdered drink mix called Fresca Vida.

To find new natural sources of food, a research team under Dr. Robert S. Harris of MIT made studies in Central America of all edible vegetation. Many of the 244 highly nutritious wild-growing food plants they discovered are now being established as garden and field crops.

The Green Revolution was slow in spreading to Latin America because farmers there often could not obtain the fertilizer and pesticides needed to maintain test crops. In El Salvador two American farm consultants hit on the idea of putting everything the farmers needed into a single package, enough to grow an experimental crop on a 100' x 100' plot. They prepared kits containing two pounds of seed, forty-two pounds of fertilizer, and six pounds of pesticides. Farmers in El Salvador snapped them up eagerly. The idea spread to other Latin American countries, where both governments and fertilizer companies are now making kits available.

But these advances are at best only palliatives. A basic solution to hunger will continute to elude Latin America until its widely multiplying birth rate is brought under control, and until land-reform programs encourage and sustain more peasants like Mariano Quispe of Peru.

11

Hunger in the United States

Deciding to investigate hunger in his own state of South Carolina in 1968, Senator Ernest Hollings toured muddy, unpaved ghettos where he saw mostly ragged women and children crowded into sagging shacks without heat, running water, or electricity. One woman with seven children told him that only two were hers; the rest belonged to friends who had simply left them with her and disappeared.

In one typical home the children had grits for breakfast, collard greens or cabbage for supper. There was no lunch. Four children were staying home from school because the other six were using the only wearable clothes.

In a shack near the governor's mansion, Senator Hollings found a sick woman who had not eaten for two days because she had had to buy her thirteen-year-old granddaughter clothes so that the girl would not be ashamed to go to school.

In Richland County he visited a slum—40 per cent white—which the local sheriff identified as responsible for almost half the petty theft and similar crimes of the area. On one street thirty-eight families shared an outhouse. Mothers in this slum taught hungry sons how to steal, hungry daughters how to earn money by prostitution.

"This is when the thought first struck me," Hollings wrote, "that it might be cheaper to feed the child than to jail the man." But Senator Strom Thurmond was not as shocked as his colleague about the hungry people in their state. "You had them back in the days of Jesus Christ," Thurmond declared, "you have got some now, and you will have some in the future. You will always have some people who are not willing to work."

According to a survey by HEW in 1969, only 50,000 out of 8,200,000 people then on relief in the United States were able-bodied men capable of work—less than 1 per cent. "The hungry are not able-bodied men, sitting around drunk and lazy on welfare," Hollings pointed out. "They are children. They are abandoned women, or the crippled, or the aged."

Dr. Kenneth Aycock, state health officer for South Carolina, estimated that there were at least 300,000 hungry people in the state—11 per cent of its population.

The South Carolina Chamber of Commerce protested that the national media were unfairly singling out the state for criticism. Was South Carolina really any worse in this respect than other states? They had a point.

"If you were to wake up one morning," wrote Gerald Leinwand in his book *Hunger,* "and read that all the people in Philadelphia, Dallas, San Francisco, New York, Seattle, San Diego, Chicago, Milwaukee, Louisville, Memphis, Houston, Denver, and Los Angeles were starving, you would not believe it. Yet, there are actually 25 million people in this country, more than the combined population of all those cities mentioned, who do not have enough money to provide them with adequate food."

A New England study observed, "Hidden away from tree-lined highways and removed from the tourist attractions, families go hungry. Unless you go looking for malnutrition you may not see it because the hungry suffer in private."

Americans, deeply moved by pictures of starving children in Biafra and refugee children in Vietnam, rushed donations to feed them. But they have often been blind to hunger in their own backyard.

Senators Robert F. Kennedy and Joseph S. Clark tried to get government figures on malnutrition in America. Surgeon General William H. Stewart admitted that he had no statistics. Asked who kept them, he replied, "That's part of the problem. It hasn't been anybody's job. We can do it all over the world, but not in the United States."

When the poor die, the cause of death is often certified as pneumonia or some other disease. But the precipitating cause may actually have been malnutrition which made the victim susceptible to infection.

Who are the hungry Americans? They are young mothers rearing children alone; families of unskilled workers made jobless by computerized machinery; young people who lack the training required by today's industry; jobless minorities crowded into city and rural slums; elderly poor struggling to survive on skimpy social security or welfare checks; Indians starving on reservations; miserably paid migrant farm workers and itinerant laborers. Among those forced to live below the poverty line are 5 million children.

The diets of the poor often lack the calcium, vitamin A, and ascorbic acid most Americans get from milk products, vegetables, and fruit. These foods are too expensive for poverty budgets that must also provide rent, clothing, medical care, electricity, gas, heat, and other necessities.

For one week *Chicago Sun-Times* reporter Anthony Monahan tried to feed his family of four on a welfare allotment. "On the third day the oranges and apples ran out," he reported "on the fifth day, the potatoes, bacon, cereal, soup, and most of the vegetables were gone—but not forgotten."

Another woman who tried the experiment said "We

admitted to being hungry a lot of the time. Our ten-year-old observed that he would be glad to be 'rich' again so he wouldn't have to fill up on bread. He showed more than the rest of us the insecurity of not knowing what the next meal would bring, and ate starches greedily."

A black housewife in Mississippi was asked which of the government surplus foods supplied for her family of ten children lasted out the month. "Well, the meat don't," she replied. "The cheese don't. The meal don't. The flour don't. The raisins don't. The peanut butter don't."

When Albany slashed welfare payments in 1969, New York families on relief had to provide three meals and every living requirement except rent for 66¢ a day per person. Yet this was generous compared to Florida and Texas, where the relief allotment per person came to only 8¢ a day.

Most Americans spend about a fifth of their income for food. The poor often have to spend from 50 to 95 per cent—and still go malnourished.

The Citizens' Board of Inquiry into Hunger and Malnutrition in the United States heard testimony in Birmingham from a middle-aged black woman from a rural Alabama county who lived on $26 a week provided by the federal Aid for Dependent Children program. Each month she used $74 to buy $108 worth of food stamps to take care of twenty children at home.

Nine of the children were her own; five were grandchildren left with her by two daughters; six more belonged to her dead brother. "You can't throw them away," she explained to the Board. "You have to take them in."

None of the children received enough to eat.

The poor try to still hunger pangs with inexpensive foods that fill the stomach but provide little real nourishment— grits, beans, black-eyed peas, potatoes, fatback. A persistent diet of such low-protein, low-vitamin foods sets up a cycle of malnutrition that carries forward from one poverty-stricken generation to the next.

Nutritionists are often upset with welfare mothers who give children sodas and cokes instead of milk. But few welfare families can afford milk regularly, while the sugar content of soft drinks pacifies the hunger of crying infants. Surviving on a monotonous diet, unable to afford recreation, the poor are far more tempted than most to drink cokes and eat candy, the only relatively cheap "rewards" their miserable existence has to offer.

Investigating hunger in Mississippi for the Field Foundation, Dr. Raymond Wheeler reported: "Slow starvation has become part of the Southern way of life. . . . The children here get up hungry, go to bed hungry, and never know anything else in between. They are hungry all the time. . . . Malnutrition impairs their performance for life."

Until 1969 American doctors believed that the severe "starvation diseases"—kwashiorkor and marasmus—were found only in Asia, Africa, and Latin America. But that year, when HEW undertook a National Nutrition Survey, Dr. Jean Van Dusen revealed that she had treated forty-four such cases on a Navajo reservation in Arizona. One typical case was an eighteen-month-old baby girl, hospitalized for swelling, irritability, and inability to eat, whose daily diet proved to be soda water, beans, and tea.

In other poverty-stricken areas the survey turned up more such cases among children examined, as well as rickets and goiter in infants under six. Fully a third of the children examined were found to suffer from anemia. There has been little improvement in the intervening years.

"Last month at Lincoln Hospital I watched helplessly as a child suffering from severe malnutrition slipped away," New York City interne Herb Schreier reported recently. "He had been brought to us too late. It isn't such an unusual occurrence."

Teachers in Head Start programs report that thousands of children arrive at school without breakfast. The Harvard School of Public Health found that more than half of

Boston's schoolchildren did not get satisfactory breakfasts, 60 per cent did not get satisfactory lunches, and less than half had satisfactory evening meals.

Doctors investigating hunger for the Citizens' Board said: "We do not want to quibble over words, but 'malnutrition' is not quite what we found: the boys and girls we saw were hungry—weak, in pain, sick; their lives are being shortened; they are, in fact, visibly and predictably losing their health, their energy, their spirits. They are suffering from hunger and disease, and directly or indirectly they are dying from them—which is exactly what 'starvation' means."

Children are not the only endangered generation. In New York City nutritionists found that many of the elderly living on fixed or limited incomes have been forced to cut back severely on food purchases because of high prices. Some chew gum in lieu of eating. One man living on $20 worth of food a month was asked how he managed to survive. "You'd be surprised how much clean garbage there is," he explained sheepishly. Living on garbage? *Americans?*

Yes. When the city of New Orleans began to charge its citizens for depositing their garbage at the city dump, the garbage inflow fell off sharply. A desperate protest against the City Hall fee came from more than a thousand people living in tar-paper shacks around the dump area. A TV reporter discovered that they were able to survive only as scavengers.

In Chicago one seventy-two-year-old man on social security was found living on a weekly ration of three tins of canned meat, a box of tea bags, saltine crackers, and two cans of soup. In Iowa a painfully thin sixty-eight-year-old widow who lived on 92¢ a day explained. "When you keep busy, you don't mind being hungry so much." Many aged Americans on welfare or social security are forced to seek food at the Salvation Army.

Faced with soaring prices at the supermarket, one senior

citizen in Washington, D.C., told Ruth Melby, director of consumer education at Friendship House, "It used to be that we went hungry the last few days of the month; now it's the last fifteen days of the month."

The sorry state of nutrition for so many millions of Americans is a major reason why we, the richest nation in the world, rank only twenty-seventh among the nations in life expectancy for men, only fifteenth for women. Our infant mortality rate is also higher than that of fourteen other countries, including all of Western Europe. Moreover, an American infant born to a poor family is only half as likely to survive his first birthday as an infant born into the middle class, and four times less likely to reach the age of thirty-five.

How has it happened that, in a land which produces such vast, often embarrassing surpluses of wheat, rice, and other cereals, we have only been able to develop into a nation described as "half-stuffed and half-starved"?

Ever since World War II the U.S. Department of Agricul-

A rich harvest may lead to political embarrassment. (FAO)

ture has supported the farm prices of American grains one way or another, to prevent an oversupply from forcing prices too low. At first the government bought and stored excess crops, holding them off the market while paying farmers subsidies to take some croplands out of production. Despite these restrictions, the use of chemical fertilizers, pesticides, and improved agricultural technology kept crop yields soaring.

Mountains of stored grain, costing the government huge sums in warehouse costs, became a political embarrassment. The farm lobby pressured Washington to get rid of the surplus. Bureaucrats feared a taxpayer uproar if grain which had cost so much money to buy from the farmers was simply dumped. So it was decided to reduce these reserves by selling or giving away grain to the hungry people in poor countries.

In the mid-fifties a program known as Public Law 480 was enacted by Congress. Under Title I of that law the United States offered grain to non-Communist countries that needed it but lacked dollars to buy it. They could pay for it in their own currency, deposited in a local bank to the credit of the United States. Most surplus American grain was sold under Title I.

Under Title II grain could be sent to any country struck by famine, flood, or other disasters, for use as part-payment of men employed in reconstruction. This aid went principally to countries willing to advance American foreign policy or military objectives.

Title III provided a Food for Peace program under the Agency for Industrial Development (AID), providing direct food relief for distribution through the Red Cross, Church World Service, Catholic Relief Service, American Friends Service Committee, CARE, United Jewish Relief, and some UN agencies.

Under Title IV countries which purchased American wheat, cotton, soybeans, butter, and other agricultural products for American dollars were given special easy credit terms.

Spokesmen for the American poor pointed out the irony of feeding the hungry abroad but not at home. Congress felt compelled to initiate a Surplus Commodity Distribution Program to provide poor Americans with unsalable foods at specified distribution centers. Each state made up its own rules of eligibility. Applicants in Maine, for example, were required to sign a four-page form ending, "I hereby swear ... that I am asking for Pauper supplies and that I am destitute and unable to take care of the necessities of life."

Surplus foods were no guarantee against malnutrition because they represented only whatever unsalable foods

Surplus food distribution. (WIDE WORLD PHOTOS)

were left over in government warehouses, not the food needed for a properly balanced diet. So in 1968 liberal pressures brought about a Food Stamp Program. Administered by state and local governments, it permitted the poor to buy food stamps at varying discounts, according to ability to pay. The stamps are good for purchasing a choice of American-produced food products at regular stores. Washington pays for all the benefits and shares the administration costs with the states.

By 1975 inflation and unemployment had made up to 34 million Americans eligible for food stamps, but less that half had applied for them. Many Americans felt embarrassed about paying for food with stamps instead of money. But most of the poor were kept ignorant of the program by state, county, and city officials opposed to its cost. Powerful ultraconservative congressmen also made sure that the federal government did little to call it to the attention of the hungry.

Even when they knew about it, poor people like seasonal farm workers, unemployed during winter months, did not have or could not spare the minimum $30 required to buy a month's supply of food stamps.

Among those who did benefit were many college students who qualified because of their negligible incomes. Typical was Pat Heiden, a junior pre-law student at Kansas University, who had been living on $4 worth of food a week that provided her with one meal a day, supplemented with apples and oranges. Using food stamps, she was able to buy $11.50 worth of food weekly. "I'm paying $700 a semester to go to school here," she explained. "My mom's working two jobs to help put me through. If I didn't have the stamps, I wouldn't eat as well."

The *New York Times* reported in 1975 that in many college communities, from a third to a half of the people receiving food stamps were students living on less than $50 a week. But there has been a great deal of public anger over the sale of food stamps to college students. "Why should blue-collar high school graduates have to support with their taxes persons who have voluntarily chosen to be unemployed for a given period of time to pursue a higher education?" demanded Congressman William Dickinson, an Alabama Republican, who pointed out that there are 11,000 food stamp recipients on the Berkeley campus alone.

In 1968 Senator Robert Kennedy charged that both the Surplus Commodity Distribution and Food Stamp programs were such well-kept secrets that they were reaching only 18 per cent of poor families. He pointed out further that 4 million poor schoolchildren were being left out of the School Lunch Program providing free or low-cost hot school lunches.

The government increased appropriations for the school lunches. But many state legislatures refused to appropriate the state's share of the cost. By 1970, 2 million schoolchildren were still missing out on the only real meal many received all day.

In Alabama one sharecropper could afford to feed his children only peas for breakfast. Speaking to the fourteen-year-old son, Dr. Raymond Wheeler found that he never had lunch even though lunches were served at school. The problem was that they cost a quarter. So the hungry boy simply sat in the cafeteria watching the other children eat. Asked how this made him feel, he replied wistfully, "Be ashamed . . . because I don't have the money."

In some schools children applying for and receiving free lunches were required to stand aside and let paying students go first. Some schools conserved funds by offering needy students free meals only on alternate days.

A school principal in the District of Columbia reported that many pupils absent because of illness nevertheless showed up at noon in order not to miss a free hot lunch, which they would not be getting at home.

Although the School Lunch Program has certainly helped

to combat hunger, it has been criticized as designed more to help farmers than children. A panel of nutritionists found many school lunches deficient in calories, iron, and magnesium, while a third lacked essential vitamins. Balanced meals are often not served because the program is used as a dumping ground for whatever foods are in surplus, to benefit agricultural prices for farmers. The children have no lobby.

One would have to be blind not to recognize that ethnic prejudice plays a part in the determination of who goes hungry in the United States, and what should be done about it. A healthful diet, like a good job and a good home, is much more likely to reward the American who looks, talks, and behaves like the majority of Americans.

In Birmingham the Citizens' Board of Inquiry found that a black applicant for food stamps had to have the signature of two white men in order to be eligible. Also, plantation sharecroppers and tenant-farmers who did not earn enough to provide food for their families all year round had to produce a statement from the landowner for whom they worked certifying that they needed food stamps.

Locked away on a reservation, the average Indian family earns only $600 a year and tries to subsist on a tiny garden grown on arid soil. Most must have government surplus foods, but lack of transportation often makes it impossible to reach the distant warehouses where they are stored. Those who can are seldom given enough to see them through the month. When this food runs out, the typical Indian meal is fried bread or beans and black coffee. The toll on Indian lives is high. For every white man who dies of dysentery, forty Indians die. Twice as many Indians die of flu and pneumonia. Life expectancy is a quarter of a century less—only forty-three years. Malnutrition is a frequent cause of death among Indian babies.

Other ethnic groups like the Mexican-Americans are

equally deprived. Subsisting on beans, tortillas, and free school lunches where available, they are subject to hunger and severe nutritional diseases. Some Mexican-American children in Texas were found to be eating clay, starch, and paper in order to ease their hunger pangs. Few Mexican-American families, investigators learned, were told of the Food Stamp Program. Luckiest were those migrant farm workers who were able to eat the vegetable and fruit crops they picked.

Because food is so expensive and ghetto incomes so meager, many of the ethnic minorities and the elderly have been driven to eating pet food, according to Jay Adelman, executive director of the New Jersey Food Council. In March 1975 up to a third of all pet food being sold in slum areas was being bought for human consumption.

Eugene Simmons, a caseworker seeking out the hungry for New York's Project FIND, reported visiting an elderly woman whose rent swallowed two-thirds of her welfare check. "As I entered her apartment," he related, "I detected the unmistakable odor of cat food frying, with a touch of onion."

In 1974 President Ford told Americans worried about skyrocketing food prices, "Here is what we must do . . . what each and every one of you can do. To help increase food and lower prices, grow more, waste less." But millions of Americans have no place to grow food and not enough to eat, let alone waste. The president also almost doubled the cost of food stamps. Millions found the savings that stamps made possible were now so small as not to be worth the time, trouble, and cost of a long bus trip to the food stamp office.

Congress refuses to allow both the Surplus Commodity and the Food Stamp program to be offered in the same place. After a dozen counties in Mississippi shifted from commodity handouts to food stamps, the state showed a drop of 95,000 people from the Surplus Commodity Program, but an

A conflict of interests. (NEW YORK PUBLIC LIBRARY PICTURE COLLECTION)

increase of only 2,500 in the Food Stamp Program. Few of the poor dropped from the Surplus Commodity Program were told about their eligibility for food stamps; and few could afford them.

More than 300 counties in the nation have refused to participate in either program. Many large-scale farmers bitterly oppose all food relief for the poor. "That's the worst damn thing you've ever done, that damn food stamp thing," one South Carolina landowner accused Senator Hollings. "If you feed them, they'll never work."

But more and more millions are being forced into the ranks of the hungry. From 1972 to 1974 food prices shot up 30 per cent. The Congressional Joint Economic Committee warned in January 1975 that unless food prices were stabilized before Bicentennial Day, fully 60 million Americans—one in four—would need and become eligible for food stamps.

By October 1975 the Food Stamp Program was costing almost $6 billion, with one American in seven a food stamp user. Charges of abuse and fraud increased, and 164 bills curbing the program were introduced in Congress in response to taxpayer anger.

Taxpayers who seek to cut food aid to the poor seldom realize that they end up paying heavier taxes for the consequences—state care of the physically and mentally retarded, and of the nutritionally crippled. To this tax penalty has to be added the heavy cost of crime and crime prevention, resulting in part from the desperation of jobless Americans trying to feed their families. The FBI estimates this invisible tax at a staggering $31 billion a year.

"It costs $10 a day to keep a prisoner in jail," Senator Hollings pointed out a few years ago. "For $10 a day a poor family can buy enough food stamps to eat for seventeen days. . . . But, of course, the average taxpayer doesn't see it that way."

The average taxpayer is taxed only slightly more than $2.50 a year for all domestic food aid programs, but over $400 for his share of military expenses. Almost no indignation is stirred by the heavy tax for the purposes of death, but intense protest is aroused over the tiny fraction of a citizen's income taxed to preserve life.

Most experts agree that our food aid to the hungry of America is tragically inadequate. "In relation to the dimensions of the problems," reported the Senate's Select Committee on Nutrition and Human Needs, "the impact of the two major Federal food-assistance programs, the food-stamp and commodity-distribution programs, has been minimal."

In 1973 the food, beverage, and grocery products industry

spent almost $6 billion on advertising and promoting foods low in nourishment—beer, liquor, coffee, soft drinks, potato chips and other snacks, candy, and sugary breakfast cereals. Americans are urged to buy them simply because they are high-profit products and easy to sell.

Meanwhile the food essential to good health—dairy products, meat, fruit, and vegetables—is priced beyond the ability of millions of Americans.

If our TV sets flashed the news tonight that a sudden famine had struck Norway, Finland, Denmark, and Sweden, we would unquestionably move swiftly to mount a massive relief effort to rush food to starving Scandinavians. Yet more people than the populations of those countries go hungry in the United States every day.

A 1970 poll by the American Institute of Public Opinion asked a representative sample of 1,500 Americans what they considered to be the nation's most serious problems. Not even 1 per cent mentioned hunger.

"Too bad that our hungry millions aren't in some other country," observed Senator Hollings dryly. "Did you ever see any commercials asking you to feed the hungry here in America? We don't want to admit we have them."

12

A Heritage of Tightened Belts

A backward glance at our history shows that hunger has been a persistent problem in every American era.

Within six months after Jamestown was colonized by 104 immigrants led by Captain Christopher Newport, 51 died of starvation and disease. Only 50 of the 102 Pilgrims who settled Plymouth survived the first winter, and the colony verged on starvation several times. It was saved once when it was able to get food from a Virginia ship found fishing offshore.

Frontiersmen who pushed into Indian country were often at the mercy of the land from meal to meal. English Quaker Morris Birkbeck, exploring the Illinois wilderness in 1817, observed of its bone-lean, hollow-cheeked pioneers, "They rely for their subsistence on the rifle, and a scanty cultivation of corn, and live in great poverty and privation, a degree only short of the savage state of the Indians."

Hunger was no stranger to plantation slaves. Even on the showplace plantation of George Washington, rations were only a peck of corn and five salt herring a week, half that for a child, and a little salt meat at harvest time. While house servants had access to their masters' leftovers, field slaves received only enough food to keep them able to work.

When the shaky economy of early American days collapsed into frequent depressions, hunger plagued the urban poor. In 1837 *New York Tribune* editor Horace Greeley found children begging in the streets of New York, skilled tradesmen pleading for waiters' jobs that paid only in food, men earning $4 a week going hungry to feed "less fortunate" men's children, and whole families dying of starvation. "Do not wait to share and increase the city's horrors!" he urged his readers. "Fly—scatter through the land—go to the Great West!" He observed bitterly, "Morality and religion are but words to him who fishes in gutters for the means of sustaining life."

A "second-hand meat saloon" in nineteenth-century Philadelphia.
(NEW YORK PUBLIC LIBRARY PICTURE COLLECTION)

The price of flour doubled, depriving poor families even of bread. A mob of angry thousands attacked a New York warehouse, seizing barrels of flour and rolling them into the street. Women scooped up spilled flour from the smashed barrels, hurrying home with it in aprons, boxes, and baskets to bake bread for their hungry families. Police who charged the flour-whitened rioters were overwhelmed and routed.

The editor of the *Commercial Register* reminded New York's elite classes that the French Revolution has begun with "mobs clamoring for bread, marching in procession, and committing outrages against the bakers." Frightened, affluent socialites hastily began organizing charity balls to buy food for the hungry poor.

Rebel soldiers in the Civil War were frequently short of food; some were chronically hungry. One Arkansas veteran who had fought in the Battle of Pea Ridge recalled, "I recollect how a pack of us young 'uns went searchin' the Yankee dead to seek for eatables in their knapsacks. . . . Funny thing was, we ended up hongrier than when we begun." Hunger also stalked the southern farms during the war, with only women and children to work the land, and afterward during the hard times of Reconstruction.

When a depression brought mass unemployment late in 1893, President Grover Cleveland resisted demands that the government take steps to feed the hungry. "While the people should patriotically and cheerfully support their government," he declared, "its functions do not include the support of the people."

In the spring of 1894 Jacob Coxey led an army of hungry unemployed to Washington to demand that Congress reverse this view by the White House, only to be arrested for "trespassing" on the Capitol grounds.

During the late nineteenth and early twentieth centuries, men, women, and children in American cities were exploited as sweatshop labor for starvation wages. Malnourished, they frequently suffered from tuberculosis and other serious diseases, dying at early ages. Legislators, representing the employer class, were slow to pass laws to protect these workers.

Hunger was a factor in the growth of the Ku Klux Klan. In 1924 journalist Charles Morrow Wilson visited his hometown of Fayetteville, Arkansas, where blacks and poor whites went hungry most of the time. Covering a Klan recruitment barbecue, he recognized many present as "among the poorer and hungrier pupils" he had gone to school with.

"I had never seen more ravenous freeloaders," he reported, adding, "I began to realize that the slobbish robe wearers, or most of them, were hungry mavericks seeking to . . . fill up their bellies. The majority wolfed and gulped like starvelings. I found myself forecasting that when the Klan 'barbecues' were discontinued, as they presently were, the membership would plummet—as it presently did."

Many of those who joined the Klan also did so to take out their frustrations as disadvantaged failures in life on scapegoats—blacks, Jews, and Catholics.

The Great Depression of the thirties brought mass hunger on a scale never known in the United States. President Herbert Hoover tried to deny the obvious to newsmen.

"Nobody is actually starving," he insisted.

But millions were. Food riots spread from city to city.

"You let this country grow hungry," warned cowboy philosopher Will Rogers early in 1931, "and they are going to eat, no matter what happens. . . . Washington mustn't forget who rules when it comes to a showdown."

In Los Angeles people whose gas and electricity were turned off cooked what food they could scrape up over wood fires in back lots. Visiting nurses in New York found children starving. The commissioner of charity in Salt Lake City reported whole families famished because local relief funds

Wisconsin dairy farmers dump their milk in protest over low prices in 1933. (WIDE WORLD PHOTOS)

were exhausted. A Kentucky coal miner declared, "We have been eating wild greens and such weeds as cows eat."

When Franklin D. Roosevelt entered the White House in 1933, there were more than 13 million jobless. Families lined up at dumps to await the arrival of trucks unloading garbage and spoiled produce. New York police donated 1 per cent of their salaries to buy food for the starving. Chicago's school superintendent pleaded with the governor of Illinois, "For God's sake, help us feed these children!" New Deal official Rexford Tugwell urged, "Never in modern times has there been . . . such moving distress from sheer hunger and cold."

Ironically, the country had never had a bigger supply of food. Agricultural overproduction made it impossible for farmers to find markets that would even pay them back just their growing costs. Many bitterly dumped surplus crops, used them as fuel, or let them rot unharvested. In the midst of this embarrassment of plenty, Americans formed bread-lines blocks long for servings of thin soup and stew.

"Don't starve—fight!" cried angry militants.

Even as Roosevelt's New Deal sought to come to grips with the problem, hungry Virginia miners smashed shop windows, looting food. Jobless auto workers in Detroit invaded self-service groceries, filled their baskets, and fought their way out.

In Arkansas when a crowd of sharecroppers marched on a general store and stripped the shelves of $4,000 worth of food, the sheriff refused to make arrests. "These ain't criminals," he declared. "And I damn sure couldn't jest start shootin' 'em down like stray dawgs. Mostly they was home people . . . fresh out of eatables and wearables, so they jest ganged up and took what they couldn't buy."

Roosevelt put Harry L. Hopkins at the head of a Federal Emergency Relief Administration. Hopkins gave one curt order to FERA officials: "Feed the hungry, and goddam fast!"

Government relief expenditures of about $1 billion a year set a new precedent in American history, establishing for the first time that food for the hungry was a government obligation, not just an optional choice for private charities.

In a desperate attempt to help farmers by stopping the glut of unsalable agricultural produce, the New Deal paid them to remove acreage from cultivation, and to destroy surplus crops and livestock. There was popular revulsion at the spectacle of plowing under crops and hogs in a hungry land.

"The fields were fruitful, and starving men moved on the road," wrote John Steinbeck in *The Grapes of Wrath.* "The granaries were full, and children of the poor grew up rachitic, and the pustules of pellagra swelled on their sides."

By 1936 the government felt compelled to amend its wasteful farm policy and convert much of the surplus into supplies for food relief. Yet even a year later Roosevelt made his famous grim assessment of the state of the nation: "I see one-third of a nation ill-housed, ill-clad, and ill-nourished." Subsequently a hot-lunch program with "penny milk" was begun for schoolchildren from low-income families, and an experimental food stamp plan was tried out.

Rearmament for war in the late thirties ended the Depression, and a war-induced prosperity continued through World War II and after it, with many fewer Americans at the poverty level. Consequently there was less pressure on Washington to feed the hungry, who became largely invisible to employed Americans. They were offered relief only from such surpluses as could not be sold abroad. During the Eisenhower administration, Republican senator John Sherman Cooper sought to get the Department of Agriculture to release some of the huge stores of cooking oils in govern-

A food stamp of the depression era. (NEW YORK PUBLIC LIBRARY PICTURE COLLECTION)

r the hungry families of Appalachia. Secretary
ison refused, insisting that they must be
verseas sales. "The primary responsibility of
artment," he declared, "is to carry out the farm
grams that benefit farmers."

During the 1960 presidential race between John F. Kennedy and Richard M. Nixon, Kennedy decried the fact that "Americans are going to bed at night hungry." Nixon replied sarcastically that this was true only because so many people were on reducing diets. Republican appeals were directed primarily toward the middle class, for whom hunger was no problem.

After his election, Kennedy postponed plans for an overseas Food for Peace Program until he had first taken care of the jobless miners of Appalachia and their families. "I can't go feeding people overseas," he explained, "without feeding the hungry in West Virginia first."

To improve the diet of the poor, he doubled the variety of foods available in the Surplus Commodity Program. But many counties refused to take all the commodities offered, and the Agriculture Department did little to promote the program. Kennedy thereupon ordered a pilot Food Stamp Program set in operation. Despite these efforts, domestic food aid programs remained seriously inadequate.

After Kennedy's death his successor, Lyndon B. Johnson, announced a War on Poverty. In March 1964 he told a group of labor leaders, "People are just not going to stand and see their children starve. . . . They will forego doing a lot of violent and improper things as long as they can, but they are going to eat." He urged union leaders to remind workers "that everybody is not eating three meals a day the way they are."

But the president's War on Poverty soon gave way to his prosecution of the war in Vietnam, into which he channeled huge national resources. Soaring inflation refuted his belief that the nation could afford "both guns and butter," compelling him to scuttle butter for guns. Hopes dashed, the poor began to protest his priorities.

In the winter of 1965–66 black families in Mississippi moved into an abandoned air-force base at Greenville, declaring, "We are here because we are hungry and cold and we have no jobs or land." They were evicted by federal troops.

The following year more than 100,000 jobless black workers in Mississippi lost their sole source of food when the state switched over from the Surplus Commodity Program to the Food Stamp Program, which few could afford. In April 1967 the Senate Subcommittee on Employment, Manpower, and Poverty went to Mississippi to hold field hearings.

"Starvation is a major, major problem now," testified Marian Wright, NAACP Legal Defense Fund lawyer. She urged, "I wish the senators would have a chance to go and just look . . . at the number of people who are going around begging just to feed their children." Some senators went.

Visiting poor counties in the Mississippi Delta, they discovered shocking cases of hunger. "I've seen bad things in West Virginia," Robert Kennedy exclaimed, "but I've never seen anything like this anywhere in the United States!"

The children were so anemic and diseased that when investigating doctors sought to move their arms and legs in tests, they cried out in pain.

Senators Kennedy and Joseph S. Clark sped a joint letter to the Department of Agriculture, the Office of Economic Opportunity, and HEW, declaring angrily, "Children dying of malnutrition, without medical care of any kind, should not have to wait one day longer than it takes their government in Washington to take emergency action."

But special welfare for poor black families in the Deep South was strongly resisted by the agricultural committees of Congress. These were dominated by southern segregationists and midwestern ultraconservatives who had little fondness for liberal proposals. Their pressure compelled Secretary of Agriculture Orville Freeman to resist the sub-committee's demand for food aid reform.

Senator Kennedy enlisted the aid of the media to arouse public opinion. *Look* magazine reported in December 1967 that some poor Mississippians "continue to exist on rice, grits, collards, tree bark, laundry starch, clay, and almost anything else chewable. Meanwhile their bodies suffer steady depletion of tissues, slow disintegration. . . . In time they become physical and psychological cripples."

In February 1968 a National Educational Television report on hunger, filmed in part on Mississippi senator James Eastland's plantation, disclosed "no food, no meat, no milk—and the children go to bed hungry. Sometimes they cry."

That month, in one of his most moving speeches, civil rights leader Martin Luther King let it be known how he wished to be remembered: "Say that . . . I did try to feed the hungry." One month later, four days before his assassination, he infuriated President Johnson by declaring, "It is morally wrong for a nation to spend $50,000 to kill a Viet Cong soldier, and just $53 a year to help a poor person in the United States."

The Citizens' Board of Inquiry into Hunger and Malnutrition in the United States concluded its investigation and told a news conference in April 1968 that it had "found concrete evidence of chronic hunger in every part of the United States." Its published report, *Hunger, U.S.A.,* estimated the number of Americans affected at 10 million. "No other western country permits such a large proportion of its people to endure the lives we press on our poor," the Board declared. "To make four-fifths of a nation more affluent than any people in history, we have degraded one-fifth merciless-ly." It sharply criticized the Agriculture Department, the agricultural committees of Congress, food manufacturers, and local and state governments for ignoring the problem.

House Agriculture Committee chairman W. R. Poage of Texas attacked the Board's findings. "The basic problem is one of ignorance as to what constitutes a balanced diet," he insisted, "coupled with . . . deliberate parental neglect [and] . . . mentally retarded parents." Many fathers of hungry children were irresponsible, Poage added, drinking away welfare money or spending it on TV sets and cars.

Congressman Jamie L. Whitten, chairman of the House Appropriations Subcommittee on Agriculture, arranged to have FBI agents seek information to discredit the Citizens' Board. One San Antonio priest protested that the FBI was harassing poor people who had petitioned Washington for food aid. Then he found himself under investigation for protesting.

Robert Kennedy endorsed the Board's investigation and summed up its highlights: "They found . . . that in the wealthiest nation in the history of the world, millions of men, women, and children are slowly starving. They found that American babies die in infancy, because their mothers cannot nurse them, and cannot buy the milk to keep them alive. They found that thousands of American children are anemic and listless, their physical growth stunted because they lack adequate protein. They found that scurvy and rickets . . . cripple American children who never drink citrus juice. . . .

"They found that hundreds of thousands of schoolchildren cannot learn their lessons, because they go to school without breakfast, have no money for lunch, and return to supper without meat or green vegetables. And they found that countless old people in America exist almost entirely on liquids, because they cannot buy or find a decent meal."

Rev. Ralph Abernathy, Martin Luther King's successor, launched a Poor People's Campaign in the spring and summer of 1968. A tent city was erected in Washington to dramatize the plight of the hungry. Mrs. Martha Grass, an Oklahoma Indian, told a Senate committee, "We shared this country with you, but you took all of it and we're starving. It's very hard when your child asks for something to eat and you've got nothing to give him, when all around you see how rich everybody else is in this country."

Poor Indians, blacks, Mexican-Americans, and Puerto Ricans complained to Congressmen that food programs for the hungry were woefully inadequate. Why, they demanded, did the government pay farmers $3 billion in subsidies to keep land out of production while appropriating only a fifth that sum to feed those without enough to eat? When they sought to stage a sitdown protest outside the Department of Agriculture, they were routed by the use of tear gas.

In May 1968 CBS broadcast a powerful television documentary, "Hunger in America," which shocked millions of Americans by its vivid close-ups of starvation in their midst. Many politicians, embarrassed by public exposure of their failure to deal with the problem, were furious at CBS.

"To admit the existence of hunger in America," Senator George McGovern observed, "is to confess that we have failed in meeting the most sensitive and painful of human needs."

President Johnson persistently rejected proposals for food aid reform from his aides and cabinet officers. If he tried to spend more to feed the poor, he pointed out, the powerful southern committee chairmen in Congress would retaliate by refusing to pass a tax bill he needed to pay for continuing the war in Vietnam. Vice President Hubert Humphrey secretly wrote to one of Johnson's close friends, hoping to enlist her help in changing the president's mind.

"It is just intolerable to me," he told her, "that there is such a problem of malnutrition and undernourishment in the United States, with our great agricultural production. It hurts the children the most, and they are the least able to bear it. . . . There are ways the President could have helped . . . but he has not."

The investigations persisted under a new president, Richard M. Nixon. In January 1969 a Senate Select Committee, chaired by McGovern, opened public hearings to air investigations of hunger by the Field Foundation, the Citizens' Crusade Against Poverty, and other concerned groups.

Dr. Robert Coles testified: "We saw homes with children who are lucky to eat one meal a day—and that one inadequate. . . . They live on starches—grits, bread, Kool Aid . . . [often] fed by neighbors who give scraps of food to children whose own parents have nothing to give them. . . . It is unbelievable to us that a nation as rich as ours . . . has to permit thousands and thousands of children to go hungry, go sick, and die grim and premature deaths."

Dr. Raymond Wheeler suggested that the white establishment in Mississippi seemed to be deliberately starving blacks into going north. Mississippi senators attending the hearing were enraged. "Gross libel and slander!" snapped John Stennis. "Totally untrue!" denied James Eastland. Dr. Wheeler, a southerner himself, invited them to visit the Delta with him to witness children's "shriveled arms and swollen bellies, their sickness and pain, and the misery of their parents."

Stennis and Eastland abruptly lapsed into silence.

In February Senator Hollings charged that southern whites had always lied about black poverty, and that people were dying from hunger and its attendant miseries in his own state of South Carolina. "I have seen it with my own eyes," he declared.

But the South was not alone to blame, he added. In McGovern's home state of South Dakota, Indians were hungry on the Pine Ridge Reservation. Nor was hunger any stranger to the Harlem constituency of another committee member, Senator Jacob Javits. The problem, Hollings said, was nationwide.

Investigating his charges against the South, reporters of

the *Charlotte Observer* found case after case of ignored hunger, like the family with five children living on rice and sardine grease. Some southern senators who felt impelled to undertake hunger tours of their own states returned to Congress calling for immediate food aid reform.

Herbert Klein, director of communications for President Nixon, accused the McGovern committee of seeking "to make hunger a political issue." Congressman Whitten argued that "Nigras won't work" if they receive free food, and that McGovern's attempts to provide free food stamps for the hungry poor were a step toward revolution. Behind closed doors angry southern senators managed to slash 40 per cent off the budget allocated to the McGovern committee.

Under heavy pressure from the committee to agree to a new $1 billion food aid bill, Secretary of Agriculture Clifford Hardin consulted the president. Nixon told him to stall with vague promises. "Use all the rhetoric," he ordered, "so long as it doesn't cost any money."

But McGovern refused to be cajoled and attacked a Nixon proposal to spend $7 billion on military hardware to protect missile sites while refusing to consider an adequate food aid program. "We can purchase with half that an end to hunger in America," he told the Senate. "I am at a loss to understand a sense of priorities which places a highly questionable antiballistic missile system above the needs of our poorest children for food which can turn them from anemic, often brain-damaged victims of malnutrition into productive American citizens."

"That hunger and malnutrition should persist in a land such as ours," Nixon conceded, "is embarrassing and intolerable." Then in August 1969 he offered a counterproposal—elimination of the Food Stamp Program, to be replaced by a Family Assistance Plan guaranteeing a minimum yearly income of $1,600 for a family of four. His critics cried foul.

The Department of Commerce had admitted that the cost

of a bare survival diet for a family of four was $1,280. Even at this level, the president's proposal would have left only $27 a month for rent, clothing, medical care, and all other expenses required for a family of four. Congress ignored his plan and merely voted to continue food aid at the level that shut out 20 million Americans who needed it.

More rhetoric in place of money was offered by the Nixon administration in December 1969 by the calling of a White House Conference on Food, Nutrition, and Health. Delegates demanded that the president free federal funds for food aid by declaring hunger and malnutrition a national emergency. They called for an expansion of all feeding programs, including a national free breakfast and lunch program in every school. The president's Family Assistance Plan was endorsed, but with a guaranteed cash income for families of more than three times what Nixon was willing to spend.

Although the government increased food stamp benefits slightly, they failed to keep pace with soaring food prices. Then, during the administration of President Ford, Secretary of Agriculture Earl Butz raised the cost of food stamps to the poor from an average 23 to 30 per cent of monthly income.

McGovern called it "the first major step backward in this country's commitment to 'put an end to hunger in America for all time.'" A study by the Community Nutrition Institute estimated that the cutback would force an additional million and a half poor people, most of them elderly, off the Food Stamp Program.

In February 1975 New York TV station WCBS broadcast a documentary revealing that more than 3 million Americans who lived within its viewing range were suffering from hunger and malnutrition.

"Food stamp administration is not working," McGovern charged, "because administrators don't feel that Butz wants it to work. Butz had complained that welfare programs like food stamps make Americans lazy. Actually, I can't think of

Long after the frontier was closed, the tradition of the individual farmer persisted in America. (NEW YORK PUBLIC LIBRARY PICTURE COLLECTION)

anything that would make a man feel more lazy or less like working than pangs of hunger."

What conclusions can be drawn from this brief résumé of the history of hunger in the United States that shed light on American indifference to the problem?

First, the early American tradition was one of pioneer stoicism. In a land of unlimited boundaries and opportunities, it was believed that any man who wasn't lazy or worthless could farm, shoot, or earn enough food to feed his family. This tradition of "rugged individualism"—each American looking out for himself—persisted even after all the land had been claimed, and after business opportunities were greatly narrowed and jobs limited.

Secondly, the frequency of depressions and accompanying hunger led many more fortunate Americans to adopt a philosophical "that's life" attitude. The hungry were expected to be grateful for whatever scraps they were fed by charity, and not look to the government for relief.

Third, the Depression of the thirties aroused concern because it was impossible to ignore the mass hunger of 13 million jobless Americans. But after two-thirds of them had been reemployed, the old lethargy about the less fortunate once more put the hungry out of sight and out of mind.

Fourth, the hungry had no powerful lobby working for them in Congress as did the agricultural interests. Consequently whatever government food the hungry received depended on what agribusiness wanted to get rid of to hold up prices. Surplus foods did not provide balanced diets for the poor, yet gave other Americans the comfortable illusion that the nation's hungry were being properly fed.

Fifth, even when the hungry began to demonstrate, march, and riot in the sixties, middle-class Americans were more upset by civil disorders and violence than by their cause. Middle America's angry response was a demand not that the hungry be fed but that a "law and order" crackdown silence and disperse demonstrators. It was in part this backlash that elected the ill-fated Nixon administration.

Sixth, Lyndon Johnson's War on Poverty degenerated into lip service when he decided to spend America's wealth on the war in Vietnam instead. During the subsequent Nixon and Ford administrations, the need for balancing the budget was the reason given for scuttling expenditures for the hungry, while military expenditures escalated to more than $100 billion a year.

Until feeding the hungry of America becomes politically popular among the nation's voters, those without enough food will probably have to continue struggling for survival on a diet of inedible rhetoric and stale promises.

13

The Politics of Food

When public emotions were aroused by the starving children of Biafra, it became good politics to vote for Biafran aid. One southern senator who did so was asked at a press conference why he had also voted against more food aid for hungry Americans. His aide offered a lame reply: "The situation is different. There's no war here."

A black reporter said grimly, "There's going to be!"

"The politics of hunger in America," observed Washington correspondent Nick Kotz in his book, *Let Them Eat Promises,* "is a dismal story of human greed and callousness, and immorality sanctioned and aided by the government of the United States."

Food relief—and the lack of it—has continually been used for political ends. When agricultural machinery displaced many southern field hands, the problem of supporting them was solved by letting counties switch from the Surplus Commodity Program to paid food stamps. Many black families were starved out of the South and onto northern welfare rolls.

Faced with the integration of all-white schools, Kotz noted, many southern counties stopped serving free hot lunches in white schools, offering them instead in segregated schools to bribe black children into remaining there.

Food aid programs are generally shaped to suit the needs of agricultural interests, not those of the hungry. A 1966 Special Milk Program for poor children came about as the result of lobbying by the National Milk Producers Association. The National School Lunch Program was likewise originated primarily as a new market for surplus crops.

The chairmen of agricultural committees in Congress operate in the interests of the corporate farms, food industries, and growers' associations known as agribusiness. They not only control all food legislation, bottling up bills they dislike, but also dominate the Department of Agriculture, whose budget is at their mercy. They have resisted every attempt to transfer food programs to the more liberal Department of Health, Education, and Welfare.

"Who'll see to it," demanded Jamie Whitten, chairman of the House Appropriations Subcommittee on Agriculture, "that [funds for food] don't go for frivolity and wine?" Whitten viewed all hunger investigations as liberal plots to win black votes by maligning the Deep South.

In 1967, when Dr. Robert Coles and three Field Foundation colleagues appealed to Secretary of Agriculture Orville Freeman for emergency aid for the hungry, they ran into the politics of food. "We were told," Dr. Coles reported, "that we and all the hungry children we had examined and all the other hungry Americans . . . would have to reckon with Mr. Jamie L. Whitten, as indeed must the Secretary of Agriculture, whose funds come to him through the kindness of the same Mr. Whitten."

Senators Robert Kennedy and Joseph Clark nevertheless managed to pressure Freeman into promising to use the Agriculture Department's $500 million emergency fund to provide free food stamps and more surplus commodities to the rural poor. When Whitten heard about it, he threatened to slash the department's budget. Freeman watered down the promised aid and returned $200 million to the Treasury unspent.

The department's emergency aid funds were spent only when an agricultural lobby needed government purchases of surplus crops to avoid a drop in prices and profits.

"We begin buying off commodities from whatever commodity group has enough muscle to get included," admitted Rodney Leonard, administrator for the food programs.

"I know that I participate in the conspiracy," observed Senator Hollings, "by filling every hungry child in America with peaches each fall when I prevail on Agriculture to buy the surplus. . . . Each senator and congressman has intermittently taken up his commodity problem with the Agriculture Department, but not the hunger problem."

Some surplus foods are also given away by the government because disposing of them is cheaper than storing them after bailing out the farmers by buying them. Food storage costs the government almost a quarter of a billion dollars a year.

Bills to increase food aid are sometimes passed because liberals tie them to farm acts the conservatives want. Thus to get legislation subsidizing cotton, sugar cane, or peanut crops, the conservatives may be forced to vote for amendments providing more food for the poor.

The public has been led to think of the American farmer as an individual entrepreneur who must be helped with all kinds of agricultural legislation in order to keep him producing the food we need. But in actual fact most farm products today are produced and controlled by large corporations.

Campbell sells 90 per cent of America's soup. Four companies divide up 90 per cent of the American cereal market. Del Monte controls fruit and Gerber baby foods. A

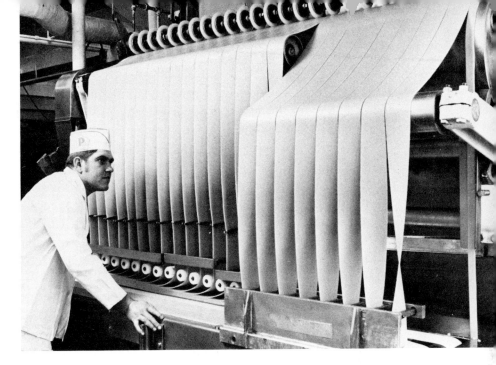

Ninety miles of cheese a day. Food production is big business in the United States and a few large corporations have great political influence. (WIDE WORLD PHOTOS)

Department of Agriculture study in 1971 found that, over a twenty-year period, only 6 per cent in the rise of food costs went to basic farmers, while 94 per cent went for increased marketing costs.

Food manufacturers are an important factor in the politics of hunger legislation. The Grocery Manufacturers' Association has been able to kill bills for increased food aid.

"We cannot find one single instance," charged Robert Choate, an official of the Citizens' Crusade Against Poverty, "of a major food manufacturer supporting a piece of poverty welfare legislation bringing adequate food to the poor unless that legislation meant increased sales for that food line."

Ralph Nader pointed out that in a single year the food industry spent only $12 million on research to make food more nutritious, but $1.3 billion on advertising. One company refused to make a new highly enriched bread its research department had developed because, while it might prove a boon to the poor, it did not provide as high a profit margin as less nutritious loaves the company sold.

Asked why General Mills did not make and market low-cost, high-protein products, executive Arthur Odell replied, "You can't sell nutrition. Hell, all people want is coke and potato chips." Some companies do develop inexpensive and nourishing synthetic foods, but only for export, keeping them off the American market to protect the considerable profits they already earn from their higher-priced food products.

Dr. Arnold E. Schaefer, director of the National Nutrition Survey, found new cases of rickets developing among American children because of a reduced consumption of vitamin D-enriched milk. The poor could not afford it; in many parts of the country it sold for up to 4¢ more a half-gallon than regular milk. "This is uncalled for," Dr. Schaefer pointed out. "It only costs a cent to enrich 1,000 gallons of milk."

The Watergate scandal revealed to Americans that the powerful dairy industry had been able to obtain increases in milk prices, costing consumers an estimated half-billion dollars a year, by pledging to raise $2 million for the campaign to reelect Nixon as president.

Lawrence I. Hewes, Jr., an agricultural economist who has served with the Department of Agriculture and the FAO, said of the secretary of agriculture, "The constituency he represents, besides U.S. farmers, includes large farm organizations, grain storage concerns, grain traders, brokers and grain exporters."

When doctors in the National Nutrition Survey warned that most Americans ate too much meat, Secretary Earl Butz promptly assured housewives that buying meat was the patriotic thing to do. He also bailed out overstocked cattlemen by making bulk meat purchases for the school lunch program, even though schools had just closed for the summer.

American food aid to the world is also highly political. The Food for Peace Program was passed in the mid-fifties to get rid of huge surpluses of grain, thus keeping prices up and saving storage costs. The export food, moreover, continues to be used as a political weapon.

The dissatisfaction of many citizens with this program was expressed in 1974 by the Anniston, Alabama, *Star:* "We dispense the surplus foods not on the basis of where they are most needed, but on the basis of power—political considerations of foreign affairs. In other words, we use the food as ammunition. . . . Very little of our Food for Peace has gone to Africa, where tens of thousands have perished from famine. But during the last year [1973] nearly half of it went to Cambodia and South Vietnam. We stopped food assistance to the Chilean people when they elected Allende, and then resumed it when the military coup ousted the Allende government."

"Food for Peace" shipments, pointed out the National Farmers Union, had become "Food for War" shipments.

In view of the dependence of much of the world on American food surpluses, the power of the United States in deciding which nations shall get food aid often determines which people shall be fed and which shall go hungry. FAO has tried to persuade Washington to turn such decisions over to a world food bank or reserve to keep them nonpolitical, without success.

The political use of food aid is nothing new in American foreign policy. In July 1921 when famine took more than 5 million lives in the four-year-old Soviet Union, then embattled by civil war, Lenin indicated the priorities for the scarce food on hand: "Feed the Red Army and the preschool children." The Bolshevik government appealed to the world for food. The American government responded through its American Relief Administration, with Secretary of Commerce Herbert Hoover in charge.

"The food supplies that we wish to take to Russia," he

explained to Congress, "are in surplus in the United States, and are without a market in any quarter of the globe." Government purchases for shipments to Russia would "give some relief to the American farmer in disposing of his surplus."

Hoover was also interested in plans for Russian relief suggested by an adviser on Russian affairs, John Spargo. Spargo wanted the food distributed only by moderate Russians, who would thereby "become the most important body functioning in Russia, and to which the people will turn naturally." Such an organization, Spargo explained, would "tend to become the real government of Russia," and would take over as soon as the Bolshevik regime collapsed.

To what extent the Spargo plan became government policy is unclear, but after the ARA withdrew, several hundred of the 100,000 Russian workers it had employed to distribute the relief food were arrested, charged with counterrevolutionary activities on behalf of the American government.

Hoover issued indignant denials, but *New York Times* correspondent Walter Duranty later wrote, "There were probably quite a number of the 100,000 Russians employed by the ARA who had abused their position somehow or other, or anyway, had done enough to warrant action by the GPU."

Although the Spargo plan failed, the American relief effort, which fed more than 11 million Russian men, women, and children at 35,000 relief stations, won official gratitude from the Soviet government, and world commendation.

After World War II, when shaky governments in Western Europe were threatened by left-wing revolution, American aid was rushed to them through the Truman and Marshall plans.

In South America the State Department operated the Alliance for Progress, which provided aid for those countries with Washington-approved governments. Correspondent

D. H. Radler observed in his book, *El Gringo,* "We really do not care what happens to Latin Americans as people; they are only pawns in the game of power politics. Our extractive industries are still here to exploit the soil and subsoil riches of the area; a large part of our aid still goes to the military."

When Juan Bosch was elected president of the Dominican Republic in 1962, in the first free elections in thirty-eight years, his left-wing views antagonized the Pentagon and State Department. Newell Williams, in charge of the Dominican AID program for the United States, vainly sought to get 30,000 tons of badly needed wheat for the island republic under the Food for Peace Program. "Ever since Bosch has been in," he told Ambassador John Barlow Martin, "we've been turned down."

No country has felt Washington's political pressure through food aid more than India, which irked the American government by its refusal to endorse the Cold War against Red China and the USSR, and the hot war against Vietnam.

In 1951, when India requested a loan to buy 2 million tons of wheat to make up a serious shortage, an amendment was tacked on to the aid bill requiring India to change its foreign policy. The amendment was only barely defeated.

"Nehru felt we were taking advantage of India's food shortage to drive a hard bargain," reported Chester Bowles, our ambassador to India. Years later, when India criticized the United States for bombing North Vietnam and sending half a million troops to intervene in the civil war, Bowles revealed that top Washington officials vowed "a food squeeze" would bring the Indians to heel politically.

In March 1966 an Indian drought sent Mrs. Indira Gandhi, the new prime minister, to Washington to plead for emergency food aid. Johnson promised to send it, but then delayed giving orders to proceed with grain shipments although tens of thousands of Indians were dying of starvation.

Bowles appealed for swift delivery of the wheat. Secretary

of State Dean Rusk replied acidly, "Tell me one thing that India has ever done for us!" Johnson abruptly canceled part of the relief shipment without explanation.

"President Johnson's decision . . . is a serious error," warned the *New York Times,* adding, "This situation leads Indians to suspect that the hold-up may be partially due to President Johnson's displeasure with Prime Minister Gandhi's recent call for a halt in the bombing of North Vietnam."

A timely gift of 100,000 tons of wheat from Canada and the purchase of 150,000 tons from Australia saved millions of Indians on the verge of starvation.

In 1975 AID reported that more than 100,000 people had died of drought-related causes in the Sahel, with another 6 million suffering from malnutrition. In Bangladesh half the population was suffering from protein and caloric malnutrition, with "a tragic toll of life among the young."

In terms of percentage of gross national product donated to the Sahel and Bangladesh, the United States ranked only fourteenth out of sixteen donor nations. Its donations to these politically unimportant regions amounted only to a fourth the food aid poured into South Vietnam and Cambodia to bolster the anti-Communist governments of Nguyen Van Thieu and Lon Nol. The 7 million people in Cambodia received five times as much food as the 75 million Bengalis in flood-ridden Bangladesh.

Until American intervention in the civil wars of Southeast Asia, that region had been the leading exporter of rice. American bombing, napalming, and defoliating the land, to deprive our opponents of cover and food, destroyed so much agricultural acreage and drove so many peasants off the land that the Indochinese needed to import rice to survive.

In the chaos that accompanied the collapse of the Thieu and Lon Nol regimes, many peasant children died of starvation. It was learned that the Thieu regime had sold $400 million worth of American gift food to finance its military spending, compounding the irony of "Food for Peace." In

Cambodia, when the Khmer Rouge rebels surrounded and cut off Phnom Penh, the CIA mounted an airlift that flew in 700 tons of munitions a day but only token amounts of food.

"Last week, a Brechtian army of impoverished women, orphans, and mutilated war veterans . . . scoured garbage pails in the back alleys for edible scraps of food," reported *Newsweek's* Tom Mathews on March 10, 1975. "Thousands of small children, their bellies swollen from hunger, lingered listlessly in the streets and, in their homes of thatch and waste lumber at the edges of the city, waited for slow death from kwashiorkor and marasmus."

Once Communist regimes had taken over in Cambodia and South Vietnam, all American food aid to their people was cut off, and no further aid was considered by Washington.

Now more than ever, all American aid was considered politically suspect in Southeast Asia. "For years," observed

U.S. aid to Southeast Asia was well publicized. (WIDE WORLD PHOTOS)

Newsweek correspondent Raymond Carroll from Laos, "AID was a symbol of the powerful American presence in the country and was widely regarded as a cover for all kinds of CIA shenanigans." In May 1975 Laotian students captured the AID compound in the center of the nation's capital and demanded that it cease operations. Secretary of State Henry Kissinger agreed to order 500 AID officials and their families flown out as quickly as possible. Deputy Information Minister Ouday Souvannavong declared that Laos would still like American assistance, but only with "no strings attached."

Four years earlier a conference of fifteen noted food experts at the Center for the Study of Democratic Institutions had warned that AID operations under the Food for Peace Program had been a fiasco: "Our record in helping the hungry countries is almost without blemish—we have consistently failed. The one place in Latin America where they have improved their food production—Mexico—would not let AID come in."

In 1974, with food shortages and inflation worldwide, the United States cut back sharply on the Food for Peace program. Fiscal officials in Washington insisted that food sent abroad should be on a cash basis, to make up for the drain on the Treasury caused by oil price hikes. Secretary of Agriculture Earl Butz also called for "cash on the barrelhead," but Kissinger argued that it was more important to use food aid as a tool of foreign policy.

Democratic senator Hubert Humphrey and Republican senator Mark Hatfield protested that most U.S. food aid was being shipped to client states and countries where Kissinger wanted to expand American influence. Food aid, they argued, should be sent abroad on a humanitarian basis only. Congress agreed, passing a rider to the foreign aid bill requiring 70 per cent of gift aid to go to those countries on the UN "most-needy" list. Butz fought back by delaying such shipments.

The Vatican representative at the World Food Conference in 1974 stated that playing politics with the lives of millions was a moral outrage. His delegation urged the wealthier nations to put their power and authority at the service of the world's poor and hungry.

The presidents of six Sahel nations appealed in vain for a "Marshall Plan" for the Sahel, to provide irrigation that would make the desert bloom and feed the region's starving millions. American aid to Africa continued to concentrate on countries like Zaire, the Ivory Coast, and Nigeria, which were rich in vital resources like oil and copper.

When American oil firms began experimental drilling in Niger, one official of that Sahelian nation said bitterly, "Let them find oil and suddenly Niger will leap near the top of African countries to which Uncle Sam gives priority." President Hamani Diori of Niger observed that American policy seemed to be "The poorer they are, the less we give them."

A secret report prepared by officials of the U.S. State Department and AID, recently declassified, declared frankly, "The United States should continue to concentrate its major economic assistance in those key African countries where the United States has major economic development or political and security interests."

Much American food aid goes to autocratic nondemocratic countries where the ruling classes oppose reform on behalf of the hungry poor. Yet Robert McNamara, head of the World Bank, declared in September 1973 that political change was essential in the developing countries. He urged swifter land reform, with new forms of rural institutions that would give as much attention to helping the poor as to protecting the power of the privileged.

Asbjorn Eide, executive director of the International Peace Research Institute, told the World Food Conference, "At present the power of a few nations is such that they can use their control over food resources to . . . use starvation or the threat of starvation as an instrument of foreign and military policy. International law must be developed to prohibit the use of food deprivation as a weapon."

Agreeing, Chinese representative Chang Hsien-wu proposed that the Third World nations be given a voice in all decisions pertaining to problems of food aid for the hungry, since they represented a majority of the world's population.

Communist representatives at the conference viewed the problem of hunger less in terms of drought than of an unfair division of the world's food, as well as exploitation of the poor masses by rich landowners and foreign corporations. With the exception of China, they supported a conference resolution calling for a cutback in military expenditures, so that these savings could be spent on increasing food production.

The United States must be part of the solution to reducing world hunger, because it is also part of the problem.

"There are many obstacles—largely political—in our own country as well as abroad," pointed out Maxwell S. Stewart, secretary of the Public Affairs Committee. "Congress does not appear to be ready to provide the necessary aid, to reform U.S. trade policy, or to actively support international cooperation among the developed and the developing countries. And the public does not seem prepared to demand such action from Congress. . . . [But] it is fair to say that if most Americans could be made aware of the daily misery facing half of the world's people, they would respond sympathetically."

Washington has yet to heed the plea of the first director-general of the FAO, Lord Boyd Orr, who urged the wealthy nations, "Take food out of politics and politics out of food."

14

Must We Pollute
Our Planet
to Save It?

Our supermarkets offer us an eye-delighting array of splendid apples, peaches, oranges, pears, plums, tomatoes, lettuce, and other produce. Such perfectly formed fruit and vegetables, unfortunately, are the result of spraying, dusting, or gassing crops with poisons to protect them from the depredations of insects. Pesticides are also used on the grains that go into our cereals and breads, and into feed for the livestock that provides our meat.

Before world food shortages complicated the picture, conservationists were becoming increasingly successful in their fight to ban the use of pesticides in agriculture. These chemicals were proved to build up harmful residues in consumers, kill up to a thousand farm workers a year, and destroy massive numbers of fish, birds, and beneficial insects. They were also condemned for polluting the air we breathe and poisoning the water we drink.

The public was shocked and aroused in 1962 by the disclosures in Rachel Carson's book *Silent Spring*. She reported that DDT was even passed from mother to embryo, so that babies were being born with poison in their systems. She also warned that pesticides were putting the balance of our ecology in serious peril. Public agitation brought about a ban on the use of DDT in American farming, and forced the chemical companies to develop less dangerous substitutes.

These substitutes have also come under attack by conservationists and environmentalists, who charge that their massive use still constitutes a threat to the ecology.

"Agribusiness and oil interests go hand in hand in exploiting the consumer for the sake of profits," stated the National Sharecroppers Fund, Inc. "True, agricultural production *has* increased since 1950. But . . . chemical fertilizers, usually made from petroleum or natural gas, have increased in use by 1,000 per cent in that period. . . . 'Modern' agriculture demands huge infusions of pesticides and chemical fertilizers, which in turn cause soil depletion, erosion, and water pollution through fertilizer run-off. As the soil declines in quality, the need for fertilizers increases, and the vicious circle continues."

The Environmental Defense Fund (EDF), which has 50,000 active members, fights the use of harmful chemicals in agriculture by lawsuits and by arguing at hearings. In 1972 the EDF filed suit to force the Food and Drug Administration (FDA) to stop farmers from fattening cattle with the chemical diethylstilbestrol (DES). They won their fight when they produced a study showing that in 100 unusual cases of cancer in young girls the cause had been traced to the treatment of their mothers with DES during pregnancy. A later court verdict, however, reversed this decision.

Agricultural unions oppose the use of pesticides in farming because they frequently cause illness, poisoning, and death among field workers. In one California case, when peach pickers went into a field a month after it had been heavily sprayed to combat the oriental fruit moth, ninety of them came down with parathion poisoning.

A pilot who flew too low spraying a crop crashed when his

wheels hit a fence wire. Unhurt but whitened by the spray, he dusted himself off and took a drink of water. He died instantly of convulsions. Ambulance attendants who carried him off became violently sick because of the pesticide on his clothes.

More than a million tons of pesticides are used around the world each year to control insects, rats, fungi, and other causes of crop damage. Their use results in almost half a million cases of acute accidental poisoning annually, generally as a result of mishaps during transportation, storage, and container disposal. Food is sometimes contaminated by spillage when shipped or stored with fertilizer.

Large outbreaks of poisoning have occurred when seed grain treated with mercurial fungicide for planting has been eaten by the hungry instead. Some highly toxic pesticides have poisoned handlers through skin absorption.

While pesticides and fertilizers help increase crops from the land, they reduce our food supplies from the water. Massive runoffs from the soil into rivers, lakes, salt marshes, and continental shelf waters have destroyed many species of fish. In many areas they poison vast quantities of shellfish, causing illness until the origin is identified and the harvesting of polluted shellfish forbidden. Herbicides are killing the plankton so important in the food chain of the sea.

"Every chemical waste or effluent, whether in air, on land, or in water, will eventually end up in the sea," warned the noted oceanographer Captain Jacques Yves Cousteau. "Of all the DDT compounds so far produced over 30 per cent are already in the oceans. We know that eventually all will end up there!"

Forbidden in the U.S., DDT is still legal in many countries overseas.

Irresponsible dumping of industrial wastes and human sewage, as well as oil spillage, adds to the poisoning of the seas.

In 1970 anthropologist Thor Heyerdahl crossed the Atlan-

This industrial complex on the Italian coast pollutes both air and water. (FAO/CAMILLO BOSCARDI)

tic in a papyrus boat. One morning a hundred miles off the coast of Mauritania, when he and his crew sought to wash their faces in the ocean, they found black lumps drifting in the water around them that was more black than blue. In midocean they again ran into a tremendous area of clotted oil, many pieces as large as apples. They couldn't brush their teeth because they dared not dip their toothbrushes in the mid-Atlantic water.

Speaking for the Ocean Resources Conservation Association, Heyerdahl warned of "the serious and global threat to marine life by pollution," and urged all governments to take immediate action to control their polluters.

Heyerdahl's alarm was echoed by Professor Troitska, a Russian oceanographer, the only woman to descend to the seabed of the Mediterranean in a bathyscaphe. For a while the bathyscaphe refused to ascend, leading those waiting above to fear for her life. When she finally surfaced, she was besieged by reporters seeking her reactions to her ordeal. "The most impressive experience I had," she said, "was viewing all that garbage on the floor of the Mediterranean!"

The Center for the Study of Democratic Institutions called for an association of Mediterranean powers to cooperate in ending pollution and harvesting more food from the sea. "The possibilities for mariculture on a very large scale need exploration, experimentation, and development," explained Dean Norton Ginsburg. "The prospects for converting the disadvantages of certain types of pollution from sewage to aquaculture and increased fisheries production requires imagination and innovation."

In harvesting the resources of the sea, however, two essential forms of energy come into sharp conflict—the need for oil for our machinery, the need for food for our bodies. Santa Barbara, California, illustrates the dilemma.

In 1969 a spill from a drilling platform off the city's beach poured 3.5 million gallons of oil into the sea, killing huge numbers of fish and birds. Outraged citizens of Santa Barbara forced an end to further drilling for oil off their coast. But by 1975 increasing shortages of oil reserves, a scarcity of jobs, and town expenses swollen by inflation forced Santa Barbarans to change their minds. To the dismay of conservationists, they suddenly voted to invite oil company operations back again.

The struggle between conservationists and those committed to increasing the world's supply of energy and food at all costs is likely to grow more intense in the years ahead.

Norman Borlaug felt compelled to oppose environmentalists and ecologists who attack the use of all agricultural chemicals—fertilizers, weed killers, and pesticides—as dangerous to the environment and wildlife. Charging that the alleged dangers were exaggerated, he pointed out that he had been working with the chemicals for thirty years without any injury to his own health.

At a Minneapolis farmers' conference in January 1971, his opposition to the ecology movement brought boos from student devotees of organic farming. He tried unsuccessfully to convince them that only chemical fertilizers could keep millions of the world's people from starving or suffering from severe malnutrition.

"I refuse to be an alarmist," Borlaug declared. "I will not bark up the wrong tree and I will not be forced into quitting on the aids we use to produce more food for man."

In another lecture he asked those who opposed any alteration of nature's ecological balance if they fully realized what such a policy would mean: "To achieve this balance you are going to have to do without a lot of things: fertilizers, pesticides, preservatives, vaccinations, prescriptions, medical care. . . . You will have to cope with disease because your intestinal parasites . . . will have as much right to exist as you do!"

At an FAO conference in Rome in November 1971 Borlaug warned, "Deny agronomists the use of fertilizers and other chemical aids and the world will be doomed—not from poisoning, as they say, but from starvation."

Fifteen noted agricultural economists, producers, scientists, and conservationists met for a five-day conference at the Center for the Study of Democratic Institutions in October 1971, to explore possible ways and means to save crops without poisoning the earth or its people.

Most agreed that the decline in the use of DDT, accompanied by an increase in the resistance of insects to other pesticides, presented a real peril to the food supply. "The insects scare the hell out of me," a scientist admitted.

Biologist Robert Rosen warned of a new threat to American grain supplies—the cereal leaf beetle. This pest has the capacity of destroying crops of spring grains totally, unless massive doses of pesticides are used. He expressed grave doubt that the cereal leaf beetle could be controlled under present pesticide regulations. In October 1974 Senator Alan Cranston raised this problem in the Senate.

At the UN, FAO director-general F. A. Boerma saw the conservationist campaign against pesticides as a serious obstacle to feeding the world. "The most important single cause of the looming crisis," he told the FAO Council, "is the imposition by developed countries of environmental controls, which, even if justified in themselves, were not accompanied by measures to safeguard agricultural production as of overriding public interest."

According to FAO estimates, despite all present uses of chemicals, insects, rats, and plant diseases destroy a fourth of the world's food supply before it reaches storage bins.

"In the Philippines and elsewhere, the ordinary field rat is still a potent foe to farmers," reported I. W. Moomaw, agricultural specialist of the Board of Directors of Agricultural Missions, Inc. "The rodents hide in hedges, and then they advance in hordes to devour the ripening ears of corn or gnaw rice plant roots. Farmers try to frighten them away with rocks and shouts, but the devastation goes on. This loss could soon be eliminated altogether if we but used the chemicals and technical weapons at our command on a large scale."

The FAO cites an outbreak of rats in two provinces of the Philippines during which farmers lost 90 per cent of their rice, up to 80 per cent of their maize, and more than 50 per cent of their sugar cane, along with huge quantities of potatoes, groundnuts, squash, watermelon, mango, and cassava. The loss threatened more than 200,000 Filipinos with starvation.

"One pair of Indian bandicoots—rats as big as cats—can

in twelve months multiply to 900," the FAO also pointed out. Rat burrows in grain storage warehouses of many developing countries consume as much as a third of the grain.

Locusts are also a serious problem. A moderate swarm is capable of eating 3,000 tons of food a day. Within one month in 1959 a locust plague in Ethiopia consumed a year's grain supplies for one million people.

Another insect against which pesticides are badly needed, according to the FAO, is the tse-tse fly. It infests 7 million square kilometers of tropical Africa, preventing valuable grazing lands from being used to raise cattle. The bite of the tse-tse transmits the disease of trypanosomiasis, which destroys cattle. If the land could be freed of the tse-tse by aerial spraying, hungry Africans would be able to count on

Locusts threaten crops in East Africa. (FAO/G. TORTOLI)

an extra 1.5 million tons of meat a year from the grazing of 120 million head of cattle.

The oil crisis of 1974–75 led to a drop of up to 30 per cent in available supplies of pesticides. Boerma warned the world's hungry nations not to depend upon the major countries for their needs, urging them instead to develop pesticide industries of their own.

Conservationists recognize the need for protecting the world's food supplies from the ravages of rats, insects, and plant diseases, but they urge greater reliance on methods less dangerous to the environment. They advocate better storage facilities of food to thwart rats; the use of biological controls against insects—the cultivation of useful insects which prey on harmful ones; and increased research to develop better disease-resistant strains of grains and foods.

Some scientists are seeking inexpensive ways to purify our polluted bodies of water. Experiments are being conducted with "living filters"—reeds, rushes, and irises. These plants cleanse water by absorbing pollutants, reducing bacteria, adding oxygen, and acting as hosts for insects and small fish that also clean up pollutants. Sudanese tribesmen have long used green plants to clean up the Nile, and in Krefeld, West Germany, bullrushes have helped purify the Rhine.

While living filters do not do a perfect job, the system is only a third as costly as conventional treatment systems. It can provide clean water suitable for drinking and fishing in regions unable to afford more expensive purifiers.

Cleansing the oceans of all the oil, industrial waste, sewage, and agricultural chemicals is going to be a much more difficult task, requiring a World Ocean Congress with international police power to stop further poisoning of the seas.

We may have an even graver problem in cleansing the

stratosphere. In June 1975, at the National Center for Atmospheric Research in Boulder, Colorado, Harvard scientist Michael McElroy revealed a study finding that nitrogen fertilizers release nitric oxide, which is destructive of the ozone layer that protects earth from the sun's most intense untraviolet rays. This complicates a problem already severe because of overpopulation—the effect on the ozone layer of hundreds of millions of aerosol-spray-can products.

McElroy estimated that the release of nitric oxide could eventually reduce the ozone layer by 30 per cent by the year 2000, possibly disrupting plant life within the sea and damaging food grains ashore, as well as increasing skin cancer. He acknowledged the importance of the $8 billion nitrogen fertilizer industry: "Our abundance of food in the United States depends in large measure on our chemical industry." But he suggested, "Philosophically, we are trying to feed too many people. Nature could have the last laugh, as we eat and die."

McElroy's revelations made front-page headlines, but he was quick to disavow any predictions of doom. He believed that greatly expanded research might enable scientists to learn how to remove the excess nitric oxide from the stratosphere.

Meanwhile, there are some silver linings in the cloud of hunger that looms so threateningly on the horizon.

15

New Ideas
for Feeding
Planet Earth

It is estimated that to feed all the people who will be on earth by the year 2000, we will need to increase the present world food supply two and a half times.

Vast areas of land not now being developed, particularly in equatorial regions, will have to be put in cultivation. In Zambia former secretary of agriculture Orville Freeman saw one unfarmed tract the size of Texas. He asked, "How many other millions of acres exist in Africa that have never been used?"

At a world population conference, eminent British geographer Sir Dudley Stamp created a stir by pointing out that the world was only cultivating about a third of its potential agricultural land, and cultivating that third quite badly.

At a Colorado conference one agricultural scientist urged that land now used for such crops as tobacco and coffee should be reclaimed for food. "You can't stay alive for long on coffee and cigarettes, although a lot of people try," he declared. "For the benefit of everyone's health, why not plant corn or soybeans in those fields?"

A "luxury" crop, tobacco (left), flourishes in Rhodesia, while wheatfields (right) in Algeria must be irrigated. (FAO/WFP/H. NULL)

There are many steep holes in the world at present unused which can be made into grazing land as highly productive as New Zealand's by cultivation and fertilization. In the humid tropics grazing crops can be grown five times faster than in well-fertilized lands in the temperate belt.

Hawaii produces five times more sugar from its cane crops than sugar beet farmers get in temperate climates. In the tropics two, and sometimes three, crops a year can be grown even with insufficient water supplies.

Worn-out soil can be made productive once more by a crash program of fertilizer production and distribution. Scientists have learned how to analyze soil and prescribe the lacking nutrients. Teaching more farmers the correct combinations of soil, fertilizer, and seed can expand crop yields. There are many untapped sources of natural gas in rural regions of the world which could provide cheap, available fertilizer.

More small-scale aids to irrigation, such as the digging of tube wells and small dams, can be built with local labor by farmers who join in cooperatives. The FAO also calls upon governments to improve and rehabilitate large-scale irrigation systems now in operation. "Through neglect, unawareness or both," the FAO reported, "a large number of irrigation systems are operating at less than 50 per cent efficiency."

The biological control of pests offers hopeful prospects for saving crops where pests have built up immunity to chemical pesticides. The leaf hopper *dikrella,* which destroys grapes and defied spraying, was controlled when California ecologists unleashed tiny wasps against them, at a saving of 87 per cent over the cost of pesticides. More research in the use of insect controls will widen their application.

The Green Revolution continues to make progress, as more and more of the world's farmers use the quick-maturing new super-seeds to plant two, three, and even four crops a year in tropical and subtropical regions. The Mexican wheats now cover seven times more acreage overseas than in Mexico itself. Some poor countries have been able to telescope into a few years progress that formerly took decades to achieve.

Canadian Frank Zillinsky, a Borlaug disciple working at a Mexican research station, has developed new tall, heavy-headed triticale hybrids—half wheat, half rye. This is the world's first new cereal grain in 10,000 years of agriculture history. A superior feed for livestock as well as nutritious for people, triticale has yields greater than those of wheat, rye, millet, or barley. Adaptable to all climates, it is thriving healthily and sturdily in countries as diverse as tropical Columbia and cool northern Sweden.

In 1974, searching for little-known edible tropical plants, the National Academy of Sciences discovered a remarkable bean plant grown as a garden vegetable in Papua New Guinea and Southeast Asia. Called the winged bean, it is

A remarkable discovery—the winged bean. Every part of the plant—pod, seeds, flowers, leaves, and roots—can be eaten.
(NATIONAL ACADEMY OF SCIENCES)

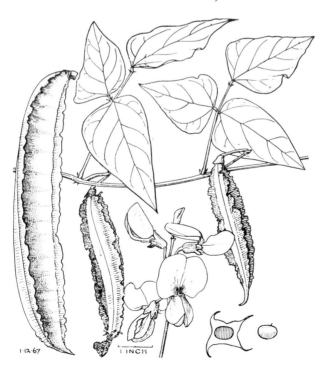

1-12-67   1 INCH

even a better source of protein than the soybean, tastes better, and, unlike the soybean, thrives in areas of high rainfall, which are among the worst for protein malnutrition. It thrives on poor soil and can grow between other crops.

Furthermore, the entire plant can be eaten, raw or cooked, with the exception of the stalk, which is an excellent animal feed. "It's like an ice cream cone—you eat the whole thing," observed Dr. Theodore Hymowitz, University of Illinois agronomist. The National Academy has recommended that the possibilities of the winged bean receive intense investigation.

British economist Ernst F. Schumacher became convinced that wealthy countries were making a basic mistake when they sought to increase crop yields in the world's rural villages by providing modern technology—expensive tractors and other large-scale agricultural equipment. Poor peasants could neither afford nor operate such complicated machinery.

American agricultural expert Charles Morrow Wilson agreed: "American farm machinery needs to be much more specialized, better fitted to particular soils and climates and crops. Most farm machinery is too cumbersome and too heavy; it drags around entirely too much unnecessary weight and fuel, and oil-wise it's too expensive to operate."

Schumacher organized the Intermediate Technology Development Group, Ltd. (ITDG), for which scientists designed simple, small, and cheap machinery—the bare essentials necessary for improving technology on primitive farms.

Ordering from the ITDG catalog, *Tools for Progress,* farmers in the remote regions of Nigeria, Jamaica, Zambia, and Pakistan can build their own water tanks for irrigation; take produce to market in oxcarts built from do-it-yourself kits; bend metal around oxcart wheels; mass-produce cheap egg trays; and make small 50-kilowatt turbines to turn pumps and engines.

A typical example of intermediate technology: Chinese farm workers with a rice-threshing machine designed and manufactured entirely in their commune. (FAO/H. HENLE)

The plan has been so successful that similar intermediary technology groups have sprung up in the United States, Switzerland, Sweden, Holland, and Germany. The Botswana government asked the ITDG to be allowed to send villagers to it for training in irrigation techniques.

"We said we do not train the villagers," Schumacher related. "If we train them they come into a European environment and will not return to the villages. They will become government clerks. But we are prepared to train the primary school teachers from the village, because they have enough motivation to go back to the village."

The spread of intermediate technology is a hopeful milestone on the difficult road toward the modernization of farming in backward regions of the world.

One nonprofit American group, Volunteers for International Technical Assistance (VITA), has 4,500 technically skilled agriculturists who do research on problems farmers in the developing countries write to them about. One VITA volunteer developed a cooking stove that works by solar heat. Easily built out of local materials, it can help poor regions where animal dung has to be used for fuel, freeing it to be used instead as organic fertilizer to increase crop yields.

Japanese agronomists have refined a technique for increasing egg production. Substituting artificial lighting for daylight, they shortened the "days" so that a henhouse would seem to have 400 or 500 in a year instead of 365. Prize hens formerly laying an egg a day promptly stepped up their output.

Americans can make a substantial contribution to a larger world food supply by substituting other forms of nourishment for the meat in their diet. It takes eight pounds of cattle feed and concentrates to add one pound of weight to cattle in the feed lot. The same land could produce instead eight times as much protein in grains for human consumption.

"The affluent must stop literally taking food out of the mouths of the poor," insisted Orville Freeman.

Food experts pointed out that even if many Americans continued to consume the same quantity of meat, they could ease world hunger by accepting slightly leaner, tougher beef—so slightly different they could hardly tell. If cattlemen would let herds graze for just two extra weeks on the open range and *then* bring them into feed lots, the experts estimated that enough grain could be saved *to feed all the hungry in the world!* And beef eating would be less hazardous to American health because the leaner beef would have less marbling of fat . . . less cholesterol.

The cattle growers were quick to see the advantage of sending more steers to market without fattening them on expensive grain in feed lots. To pressure consumers into accepting the less tender meat, they won agreement by the Department of Agriculture in March 1976 to upgrade it as "prime" and "choice." The feed lot savings were not passed along to the consumers, however, increasing growers' profits instead.

The Consumer Federation of America went to court to protest the change, but it lost its case. Less American grain is now being used to fatten cattle, but whether this development will reduce world hunger remains to be seen.

We should also consider accepting other kinds of meat we are not accustomed to buying. Warner Boehme, a spokesman for the rendering industry, points out that the American meat industry wastes valuable sources of protein and B vitamins by discarding calf brains, pork liver, and lamb liver as unsalable. Yet calf brains, for example, have long been considered a gourmet delicacy in Europe.

In Southern Rhodesia nine large cattle ranches are now harvesting such wildlife as eland herds. In East Africa antelope is being bred as a new source of meat. Somalia is exporting camel meat to Saudi Arabia, while Uganda and Kenya are butchering surplus hippos and elephants.

Science has also developed analogs—attractive meat substitutes. Imitation ham, steak, or chicken, made of vegetable protein fibers spun in mills, look and taste like the real thing and are more nourishing. Meat substitutes may soon become as acceptable to consumers as oleomargarine became to butter lovers. One bacon substitute made of soybeans is not only high in protein and low in cholesterol but also needs no refrigeration or cooking.

Analogs may become the transitional foods to make more people vegetarians, saving vast feed-grain fields to produce crops for human consumption.

More experimentation is needed to develop leafage as a source of protein. India has made large-scale trials of protein extracted from leaves of the "drumstick tree" as a dietary supplement. In Nigeria twenty-six children suffering from kwashiorkor who were given a daily supplement of leaf protein recovered within ten days. The FAO notes, "There has been surprisingly little research on the practical usefulness of this potentially enormous source of protein."

In Rome, Paris, Berlin, Singapore, and Moscow, restaurants are offering their customers the tuber roots of bellflowers as a choice rampion salad. Chinese, Russians, and Israelis eat the flavorsome, highly nutritious tuber roots of sunflowers.

Water plants like seaweed and algae are excellent sources of protein, but so far no way has been found to make them palatable. Professor Nevin S. Scrimshaw of MIT nevertheless believes that the acceptance of new foods is a matter of cultivated taste. He has pointed out that the maguey worms, termites, locusts, snakes, and rats considered delicacies in some regions of the world would make Westerners gag, while Western caviar, artichokes, truffles, Limburger cheese, snails, and blood sausage would be just as difficult to introduce into societies which are not accustomed to them.

"One of the hardest tasks of my life," Scrimshaw related, "was to convince the population of a small Guatemalan village wholly unfamiliar with milk that the dried skim milk provided by UNICEF would not make their children sick. ... Most of the processed foods of Europe and America were not even available a generation ago. Within the life span of a single generation, many new and substitute foods have become conventional."

The same, he is convinced, will become true of many other nutritious new sources of protein now being wasted, as they are introduced into the world diet of the future, though it should be noted that some people are allergic to milk or physically unable to digest it.

To fight malnutrition, inexpensive new foods have been developed that come as close as possible to offering all-purpose high-protein diets. Turkey produces a new low-cost weaning food called Sekmama. Made of wheat flour, chick pea flour, soya (soy) flour, dry milk, and sugar, with added vitamins and minerals, it is fortifying infants against the malnutrition that affects 8 million preschool and school children in that country.

In Hong Kong schools today Vitasoy, a mildly carbonated drink with a soybean base and high protein content, outsells all other carbonated drinks. Acceptance was won for it by an advertising and promotion campaign as insistent as those in this country promoting colas and soft drinks. In South Africa protein-enriched soft drinks and candy are being marketed under the trade name Pronutro. Jamaican babies are thriving on concentrates made half of milk and half of protein supplements derived from leaves.

American scientists at Purdue University have developed a new type of protein-rich sorghum, the fourth biggest cereal crop in the world and the chief diet staple of 10 per cent of all people on earth. The new variety is three times as potent in promoting body growth as ordinary sorghum, and grows well in temperate climates.

With the demand for soybeans outstripping the supply, Spiros M. Constantinides, professor of food at the University of Rhode Island, found an excellent substitute in ripened okra seeds, pressed, dried, and ground into flour. Unlike soybeans, okra yields two crops a year and needs less fertilizer.

At the Michigan Agricultural Experimental Station, director Dr. Sylvia Wittwer developed new varieties of peas and beans that pluck nitrogen—a building block of protein—out of the air. Both crops, Dr. Wittwer averred, could lower food prices and help end world hunger.

For some 300 million people around the world, corn is the staff of life. But corn is poor in protein. A Rockefeller Foundation team of scientists has now developed a mutant corn called Opaque 2 which is as protein-rich as skimmed milk and can increase body weight twice as fast as ordinary corn. Ridding the corn of its one drawback, a bitter taste, the experimenters found that it could also reverse the ravages of protein starvation in malnourished children. American farmers planted 200,000 acres of it in 1974, and it is now being grown in significant quantities in several countries. "Scientists calculate," declared Dr. Ernest Sprague, head of the crash project to perfect the super-grain, "that with just this corn, plus a few supplementary vitamins, an adult could eat adequately for ten cents a day."

Another promising new food is hasawi, a strain of super-rice being developed in Saudi Arabia by a team of Taiwanese agriculturists. More nutritional than any other strain of rice on earth, it is in great demand by the Saudis, who pay more than twice as much for it as for ordinary rice. Its drawback is that it is photosensitive, flowering only in winter when the days are short. Crossbreeding experiments are developing a strain that will also make it possible to plant hasawi for summer and fall harvests, reducing its cost.

Malnutrition in the United States is to some extent caused by the wrong food, not just the lack of it. The Nutritional Action Organization observes that our leading food corporations produce many non-nutritious products which "epitomize what is wrong with the American food supply," contributing to such major health problems as obesity, intestinal cancer, heart disease, and tooth decay.

According to Dr. Aaron Altschul, special assistant for nutrition improvement at the Department of Agriculture, food manufacturers have the ability to fortify bread and cereals so that every child in the nation could have sufficient protein, at a cost of only 22¢ a year per child.

They have produced CSM for the department's overseas food aid programs, pointed out Dr. Richard Hull, vice chairman of the White House Conference panel on food quality. CSM, made from corn, soy flour, and dried milk, supplies every nutrient and 70 per cent of the calories needed by children. Half a million pounds of CSM were distributed to poor children around the world in 1967 at a cost of only 2¢ per child. Why not here?

Because pressure from the milk and milling industries' lobbies led the Food and Drug Administration to restrict the sale of such low-cost fortified foods in the United States.

American food companies can also produce sugarless bread that is 3¢ cheaper, 50 per cent higher in protein, and less fattening than commercial bread. It also tastes better and works better in toasters. Karl Finney of the Department of Agriculture's Marketing Research Center in Kansas has been making it experimentally. "We haven't found anyone who would take sugar bread after they tried nonsugar bread," he reported. But it has still to be produced commercially.

The sea's declining harvests of commercial fish make it imperative that we seek a Blue Revolution to match Borlaug's Green Revolution. According to Elisabeth Mann Borgese, author of *The Ocean Regime,* the technology exists to transform the whole system of farming the seas.

Dr. John Ryther of the Woods Hole Oceanographic Institute pointed out that there are about one billion acres of coastal wetlands in the world where fish, oysters, and other seafood could be bred in nurseries at very little cost. "If only one-tenth of the available wetlands . . . were set aside for aquacultural development," Ryther declared, "the potential yield, using improved methods of production, would be 100 million tons a year—the equivalent of the potential yield from the world's commercial fisheries."

Some authorities go even further, maintaining that a protein crop equal to three times the world's food catch from the sea could be raised from mussels grown in Long Island Sound alone, provided the water there were cleansed of pollution.

Fish farming goes back to Greek and Roman times, when Aristotle wrote about raising oysters. Japan, which derives 13 per cent of its ocean food from mariculture, has been able to multiply its oyster production 100 times by growing oysters instead of just harvesting them in a natural state.

Colin Clark, former director of Agricultural Economics Research Institute of Oxford, reported in 1970: "Some very interesting work is going on in farming fish in ponds in hot climates, where the water is fertilized to promote the growth of plant plankton, and further nutrients are added to the water to feed the fish. . . . Yields of 2 tons of fish per hectare [2.5 acres] per year have been attained. . . . This seems an obvious method of remedying protein shortage, at any rate in tropical climates."

The world's supply of fish protein could also be vastly increased if fishing trawlers would not throw back into the sea varieties which at present are not regarded as salable.

A full catch of hake, off the coast of Valparaiso, Chile.
(FAO/S. LARRAIN)

The magazine *Resources* notes, "By utilizing the unharvested fish in United States waters alone, enough fish protein concentrate can be obtained to provide supplemental animal protein for one billion people for 300 days at a cost of less than half a cent a day per person."

Donald R. Whitaker of the National Marine Fisheries Service points out that with every pound of shrimp netted by Gulf of Mexico trawlers, five to ten pounds of fish like croaker are hauled in and dumped as unsalable. We could have enough fish to feed hungry Americans for the next several years if they would learn to eat squid, skate, croaker, hake, and other species not now customary in our diet. The Soviet Union, in fact, is pioneering in the processing of ocean plankton and krill, the food of whales, into food for human consumption.

Working with the Seri Indians on the Gulf of California, botanist Richard Felger and a team of anthropologists found an important part of their diet to be seeds of eel-grass, the marine plant *Zostera marina,* which are ground into an excellent bland flour. This "grain of the sea" could become an especially valuable food of the future because harvests require no fertilizer or fresh water to cultivate.

Techniques of increasing crop yields, taught to more of the world's poor farmers, can be an effective weapon against hunger. Sartaj Aziz, director of FAO's Commodities and Trade Division, suggests that China's collective way of farming may be an important wave of the future: "One has only to study Israel's kibbutz and Tanzania's 'Ujamaa' to discover the scope that exists for adapting at least some of the basic principles revealed by the Chinese approach towards rural development."

Israel has introduced a new system of drip irrigation which dribbles water at the rate of a gallon an hour directly to the plant roots, instead of spraying up to sixty gallons an hour into the air or furrows, where perhaps half evaporates.

Today drip emitters based on Israeli patents are being mass-produced in the United States. They are sold around the world, creating bumper harvests while holding down irrigation costs.

In California fertilizer is added directly to the water in drip emission, with spectacular results. Fruit trees that normally take four years to bloom now bear fruit in two. Drip irrigation, however, represents a leap forward only for well-to-do countries that can afford the system, which costs $600 an acre to install, as against $700 for sprinklers. Neither is an answer for poor countries which are compelled to continue irrigating crops in the ancient ways.

Many religious groups believe, as from time immemorial, that prayer can influence harvests. In Dayton, Ohio, Dr. Gus Alexander, specialist in communications research at Wright State University, led members of the Church of the Golden Key in an experiment. Prayer sessions were held in half of a dozen soybean fields every night for forty nights. Dr. Alexander reported that the harvest from the prayed-for fields outyielded the others by 4 per cent. He believes, "If we put it to use, our psychic abilities—our abilities of prayer—could vastly improve the world's food supply."

One major problem in feeding the rural poor of the world is just making sure the food gets to them in good shape, and this problem of preserving food is aggravated by transportation difficulties due to poor or nonexistent roads. Cereals and other foods are subject to mildew, fungus, and contamination, and the FAO estimates the loss of perishable fruits and vegetables at up to 40 per cent. Some food companies are now processing large cans of dehydrated food which can be restored to its natural state when the consumer adds water. The advantages are savings in transportation costs, an 80 per cent reduction in storage space required, protection against rats and insects, and a preservative life of up to twenty years, making these foods ideal for food reserve banks.

Most of the world's farmers would like to modernize their operations, but cannot do so without credit. An FAO study found that only 5 per cent in Africa, and less than 15 per cent in Asia and Latin America, receive such credit. Moreover, all but a fraction of these are the bigger landowners.

The FAO recommended the establishment of a World Food Council to finance and coordinate all programs for increasing food production, building food reserves against emergencies, and distributing it to countries in need. Each nation would contribute 15 per cent of each year's crops to the reserves.

These proposals, in essence, were adopted by the UN World Food Conference in Rome in November 1974, and by the UN General Assembly a month later. The World Food Council was set up and held its first meeting in June 1975. Work to establish an International Agricultural Development Fund, a Consultative Group for Investment and Agricultural Production, and a system of international food security reserves resulted in considerable progress by the fall of 1975.

Many American farmers opposed the food reserves plan, fearing that surplus production would depress farm prices. But Norman Borlaug suggested, "If all nations come together we can find some way to finance such a reserve, to take these horrendous gyrations out of supply and prices." He urged a World Food Bank with international warehouses in strategic locations around the globe for swift relief of famine.

Such life-saving food stations would prevent the catastrophes caused by months of delay in shipping food halfway around the world. "It is an indictment of the human race," Borlaug charged, "that we have a world bank for money, but not one for food."

Many overweight Americans are reaching the conclusion that they ought to diet or fast, for the sake not only of their health but also of their conscience.

Senator Mark Hatfield gave a 67-calorie luncheon for Washington officials to offer them a taste of the daily ration in starving nations. The U.S. Senate subsequently passed a resolution urging Americans to save food through fasting. And just one less hamburger a week, Senator Hubert Humphrey pointed out would release 10 million tons of grain a year.

In 1974–75 the National Conference of Catholic Bishops called for two days of fasting a week. The Quakers passed out pledges to reduce meat consumption by a third.

The National Council of Churches organized the Community Hunger Appeal, sponsoring 1,500 "hunger banquets" across the country. After a thirty-hour fast, guests gathered at churches for a banquet at which a third were served a steak or chicken dinner, another third received a "refugee diet" of blended corn and soybeans, and a third were fed a starvation diet of rice and broth. The different menus were symbolic of the divisions of food for the people of the world. At most dinners the guests decided to share the steak or chicken equally, even though it meant smaller portions for everyone.

Secretary of Agriculture Earl Butz objected to the urging of "ill-informed, fuzzy-thinking do-gooders" that we "cut back our livestock production to meet world food needs." He insisted, "Americans are not going to eat one *less* hamburger per week. They are going to eat one *more* hamburger per week. Furthermore they need have no sense of guilt."

Americans had a choice of that assurance or the conviction of Michael Harrington, a former presidential adviser on poverty who asserted, "It is an outrage that even as children starve in Bangladesh and Chad, millions of Americans are suffering from overweight."

16

Controlling World Population

When Japan invaded China in the 1930's, the Japanese government justified its aggression by the fact that too many Japanese were crowded into too small a territory. Similarly, when Hitler first began conquering nations around Germany, he offered as his excuse the need for *lebensraum*—room to live. Mussolini, attacking Ethiopia, told Italians it was needed as a colony in which to settle Italy's surplus population.

Although these alibis were patent pretexts for aggression, it *is* true that governments with more people than they can properly feed are often tempted to spill the surplus over into other countries. Land may be opened for them by conquest if they are not permitted to settle in other nations.

Aware of this danger, the wealthy nations have offered food aid to the world's hungry countries. But they have been distressed to find two-thirds of this relief swallowed up by an exploding birth rate. Even though food production has increased substantially, world population has increased faster.

By 2000 A.D. it will be over 6 billion, and may be nearer 7 billion," C. P. Snow has predicted.

Each time your heart beats, three more new hearts start to beat elsewhere on earth and three more mouths must be fed. Borlaug has warned, "If population continues to increase at the [present] rate, we will destroy the species."

There is general agreement that curbing the numbers of people the earth has to feed is an urgent priority. The Green Revolution has simply bought us time to bring them into balance with world food supplies. If this is not done volunatrily, food experts warn, it will come about through mass starvation. In Borlaug's opinion, "To do nothing and rely upon the Malthusian principle to stabilize numbers through starvation is immoral."

In June 1975 the World Food Council estimated that 400 million people on earth were still starving or undernourished.

The situation in southern Asia is already hopeless, according to Philip Handler, president of the National Academy of Sciences, and American aid by itself can only make things worse. "Cruel as it may sound," he declared, "if the developed nations do not intend the colossal all-out effort commensurate with this task, then it may be wiser to let 'nature take its course' as Aristotle described it: 'From time to time it is necessary that pestilence, famine, and war prune the luxuriant growth of the human race.'"

This school of thought regards gifts of food aid to the overcrowded poor countries as mistaken generosity because "the more we feed, the more they breed," compounding the problem. It argues that if people breed like rabbits they must be allowed to die like rabbits, until gradually improving education and the demand for a higher standard of living teach them the necessity of population control.

Dr. A. V. Hill, Nobel laureate for medicine and former president of the British Association for the Advancement of Science, thinks our humanitarian impulses might quickly shrivel up if overpopulation began affecting our own way of life: "Suppose it was certain now that the pressure of increasing population, uncontrolled by disease, would lead not only to the exhaustion of soil and other capital resources but also to the continuing and increasing international tension and disorder, making it harder for civilization to survive, would the majority of humane people change their minds?"

But Lord Ritchie Calder has seen a moral flaw in Hill's reasoning: "The ruthless logic to be derived from A. V. Hill's rabbit analogy would be to invent a human myxomatosis [a disease artificially introduced into Great Britain to destroy the rabbit population]. 'We' would kill 'them' off like beasts, battening on 'our' civilization, wasting 'our' soil, and squandering 'our' capital resources. But who are 'we' and who are 'they'?"

The problem is not merely one of reckless breeding, but

"We" and "they." (RESCHKOV/WINDSOR STAR)

also of a declining death rate caused by modern medicine. In India, for example, a girl born today has a life expectancy of forty-eight years, whereas her mother's life expectancy at birth was only twenty-seven years. Not only does she therefore have a longer reproductive span, but her children are more likely to survive, increasing the population geometrically.

All the more reason, argue those who oppose food aid, why trying to save millions on earth doomed to starve is an exercise in futility. The food supply can be increased, but not stretched out ad infinitum. Right now, if everyone on earth shared all available food equally to the last grain and animal, everyone would suffer from protein deficiency.

Opponents of food aid argue that the United States, for the sake of its own future generations, should refuse to accept responsibility for feeding all of the world's starving, remaining an island of plenty in a sea of hunger. Ebenezer Scrooge expressed their view bluntly in *A Christmas Carol:* "Let 'em die and decrease the surplus population."

Most Americans are repelled by such cold-blooded logic, and feel morally obligated not to turn their backs on human suffering. But many are also becoming impatient with food-poor countries that continue to have bumper crops of babies.

In November 1974 irate congressmen introduced a bill to cut off all U.S. aid to "any country which the President determines is not making reasonable and productive self-help efforts, especially a family-planning program designed to control population growth." Orville Freeman summed it up: "The choice is . . . between famine and family planning."

But a major obstacle to convincing people of the poorer countries that they ought to limit the size of their families is the high death rate, which is still a problem in many countries despite a downward trend. Many poor peasants have eight children in the hope that at least three will survive to help them farm and to take care of them in their old age.

A report to the World Health Organization from India explained: "It is generally held that contraception, including irreversible methods [sterilization], is more easily adopted if it can be convincingly shown that the children already born are going to survive. . . . Response to family planning efforts will certainly depend, to a very great extent, upon how people view their children's prospects of surviving to adult age."

Dr. Nevin S. Scrimshaw of MIT considers it futile for the United States to attempt to hold down world population growth by offering food aid to the hungry nations only on condition that they sponsor family-planning programs. "Because a reduction of the high mortality among young children is an important prerequisite for the success of family planning," he has declared, "there is a strong argument for combining family planning efforts with those health measures that will reduce such mortality."

In the race against hunger, food experts think it might be possible to increase food production by 1 to 1.5 per cent a year. But the birth rate continues to increase at the rate of 2 per cent or more a year. Countries with a birth rate of more than 3 percent annually include Algeria, Colombia, Kenya, Mexico, Peru, the Philippines, Rhodesia, Syria, and Zaire.

The influence of the Roman Catholic Church remains a strong deterrent to birth control in Catholic countries, particularly in Latin America. The Vatican accepts the goal of planned parenthood, but only as long as it is not achieved by the use of any kind of contraceptives, which it considers a violation of natural law.

Preparing to go to Oslo for the Nobel award in the fall of 1970, Borlaug was asked to stop off at Rome to address an FAO conference to be opened by Pope Paul. He said, "I know well where the pope stands on population, and it is not where I stand."

The proposal that the American government provide birth-control help for poor nations was first made during the Eisenhower administration. The president opposed it, telling the press, "This Government has not and will not . . . as long as I am here, have a positive political doctrine in its program that has to do with this problem of birth control. That's not our business." Later, out of office, he explained that as president he had not wanted to "violate the deepest religious convictions of large groups of taxpayers."

Ironically, it was America's first Catholic president, John F. Kennedy, who warned Congress in his first foreign-aid message that such aid would be meaningless unless the countries receiving it agreed to take steps to reduce their annual crops of babies.

Eisenhower now agreed. "It does us little, if any, good," he declared in 1963, "to provide economic or technical assistance to nations which show no concern for their population explosion."

In March 1965 the U.S. Agency for International Development was authorized to begin training social workers of poor countries in family-planning methods. They were furnished with funds, transportation, and materials for carrying out a nationwide educational program. Two years later AID made the first grants to participating countries for the purchase of contraceptives to be used in the program.

In India special vans with loudspeakers tour the country, announcing the arrival of family-planning workers. Remote villages are reached on traveling elephants bannered with a red triangle, the family-planning symbol. Playlets are presented to emphasize the program's slogans, "A small family is a happy family," and "One, two, three—stop."

Many of the workers are nurses and midwives who travel around rural India giving family-planning classes to village wives along with advice on child nutrition. Women are encouraged to limit the number of their children so that they will be better able to care for those they have. In many villages, family health centers provide contraceptives and also offer vasectomies to fathers of three or more children.

This simple operation, which takes no more than five or

A poster in India urges that "two or three children is enough."
(UNICEF/ABIGAIL HEYMAN)

ten minutes, results in permanent sterility in a man without affecting his sexual activity in any way. Many Indian states provide cash incentives, paying a bonus of about $25 to volunteers who agree to a vasectomy with the consent of their wives.

Many private organizations are also involved in providing countries that request family-planning assistance with specialists, laboratory equipment, and supplies. They include the Population Council, the Planned Parenthood Federation of America, the World Population Emergency Campaign, and the International Planned Parenthood Federation.

Among the governments with active family-planning programs today are India, Pakistan, Japan, China, Nepal, Thailand, Sri Lanka, Malaysia, Indonesia, Taiwan, Hong Kong, Singapore, South Korea, Turkey, Egypt, Tunisia, Morocco, the Philippines, Jamaica, Barbados, Chile, and Venezuela. Perhaps the most successful has been Japan, which has reduced its birth rate from 3.4 per cent to only 1.1 per cent today.

At the UN World Population Conference in Bucharest in 1974, however, when the United States sought to assign a large share of the blame for the food crisis to the population explosion in the poorer nations, angry opposition was aroused among Third World and Communist countries. They charged that the major problem was overconsumption by the developed nations. They also accused the United States and Western Europe of seeking to hold down Asian, African, and Communist numbers for purely political and military reasons.

President Nicolae Ceausescu of Communist Romania announced his government's determination to increase its population by 25 per cent by 1980. Denouncing birth control, he insisted that modern agricultural science could increase food yields enough to take care of growing world needs.

The Indian delegation declared that it did not consider family planning a sufficient solution to the food crisis unless it was also linked to a dramatic redistribution of wealth between rich and poor nations.

The Soviet policy had been expressed by Nikita Khrushchev as far back as 1954, when he declared that even if another 100 million people were added to the USSR's population, "it would be too little. The more people we have, the stronger our country will be."

Although Mao Tse-tung expressed a similar belief about the Chinese, China has quietly accepted family planning, and has dropped its growth rate to 1.8 per cent. An unconfirmed report tells of the Chinese government's curtailing of food rations during 1966, a year of drought, for families with more than three children, to encourage smaller family units.

The Algerian delegation insisted that the world's major

problem was not curbing the populations of the hungry nations, but "curbing the appetites of developed countries" so that there would be enough food to go around.

"People tell us that unless we cut down our population growth we will starve," Dr. Obi Chizea of Nigeria said scornfully. "But you cannot scare us by saying we will die of hunger because we die of hunger every day."

UN secretary-general Waldheim warned, "The next thirty to thirty-five years may well be the most challenging in the history of mankind . . . for it is virtually certain that the world's population will double." Never before, he pointed out, have "nations or the international community been faced with such expanding demand for food, shelter, employment, education, and health care." He urged joint "immediate action" by all nations to rise to the crisis and surmount it.

The American delegation pointed out that food reserves were running low even in North America, the world's breadbasket. The world, said U.S. delegate Christian A. Herter, Jr., "may be able to manage today and next year on food, although only at a minimal dietary level for a substantial percentage of the people, but what of ten years from now, or twenty-five years?"

The United States called for a gradual decrease in world population, until by the year 2000, families would be limited to a maximum of two children. From then on the population would only replace itself. Great Britain supported a key American proposal that birth-control knowledge be made available to every couple in the world by 1985.

"What we need," said Orville Freeman, "is zero growth rate everywhere—and as soon as possible." He urged adoption of a four-point program which was being applied successfully in China and Singapore: (1) making family-planning services available to everyone; (2) meeting the basic economic and social needs of the poor so that they lose the motivation that drives them to have large families; (3)

developing new prestige roles for women other than through bearing and rearing children; (4) instituting government policies to encourage and promote a low fertility rate.

Economists estimate that it could cost almost $1 billion a year to help overpopulated countries reduce the 75 million "too many" births every year that intensify the world's hunger problem. This would require only a tenth more aid than the developed nations are already providing these countries.

Johnson C. Montgomery, a founder of Zero Population Growth, Inc., sought to set an example for fellow Americans and other world parents by seeking a vasectomy after he and his wife had had two children.

"Don't ask me to cut my children back to the same number of calories that children from large families eat," he declared in a *Newsweek* column. " . . . Nancy and I made a conscious decision to limit the number of our children so each child could have a larger share of whatever we could make available. We intend to keep the best for them. . . . Why should we share? The nations having the greatest needs are those that have been the least responsible in cutting down on births. . . . As compassionate human beings, we grieve for the condition of mankind. But our grief must not interfere with our perception of reality and our planning for a better future."

In 1975 proponents of zero population growth introduced a counter-celebration to Mother's Day, calling it *Non-Mother's Day*, in honor of those women who have made deliberate decisions to forgo having children. Apparently more and more American families are making this decision, because the government revealed a falling birth rate for 1975, to the point where Americans were simply replacing their own numbers.

When the day of large families is over in the poor nations as well, victory over hunger on planet earth might be possible for the first time in the history of the human race.

17

The Race
Against Time

"We are in a race against time to keep from starving," Norman Borlaug warned in 1973. If we simply ignore the problem, we may condemn ourselves and those who follow us to a subhuman existence, short of food and space. The more densely packed the world of tomorrow, the more unbearable will be the lot of all its citizens.

We must win the race between population and food, or the developments envisioned in the first chapter may move out of the realm of fantasy into that of fact. But the task is formidable. We are failing to feed all of our 3 billion fellow passengers on planet earth right now. Will we be more successful by the year 2000, when their numbers may have exploded, assuming the present rate of expansion, to 7 billion? Or only 30 years later, when there would be *14* billion mouths to feed?

The prestigious Club of Rome, whose members analyze future world problems, has concluded: "Because our environment—the earth—is finite, growth of human population and industrialization cannot continue indefinitely. This fact must be impressed on the population—for it is not generally recognized how very close we are to the physical limitation which defines the carrying capacity of the globe."

We have been warned repeatedly. Back in 1965 Senator George McGovern predicted, "Major starvation will be the most painful fact on this planet within ten years." Noted Swedish economist Gunnar Myrdal agreed, adding somberly, "I am frightened." Professor Robert C. North, Stanford political scientist, observed, "The twin problems of expanding population and contracting resources dwarf all other problems. . . . This awesome time bomb . . . ticks away."

The time is growing too short for typical bureaucratic responses—acknowledging the problem, establishing committees to study it, then filing and forgetting their reports as the public attention is diverted to some new crisis.

In 1974 the Senate Select Committee on Nutrition and Human Needs took testimony from several hundred doctors, dieticians, educators, food manufacturers, and consumer representatives, then drew up a report showing how the United States might best produce and distribute food to end world hunger and malnutrition. The report ended up gathering dust in the Library of Congress.

"Very few grasp the magnitude of the danger that confronts us," Thomas M. Ware, head of the Freedom from Hunger Foundation, told the Senate Select Committee. " . . . The catastrophe is not something that *may* happen; on the contrary, it is a mathematical certainty that it *will*."

The American government's priorities were questioned by Professor Seymour Melman, of Columbia University, who made a study of military costs. He asserted that for the $5 billion cost of producing the problem-plagued C-5A military aircraft, hunger could have been eliminated entirely in the United States. For just one month's average cost of the Vietnam War—$3.5 billion—the country could also have trained 100,000 agronomists or endowed four new Rockefeller Foundations for the fight against hunger overseas.

England's Lord Boyd Orr has estimated that just 10 per cent of the total budget spent on world armaments could end malnutrition on the face of the earth. And in a very real sense, every nation's security is far more threatened by world hunger than by political rivalry.

Lester R. Brown of the Overseas Development Council declared in his book *Seeds of Change,* "Our foreign policy, and our relations with the world today, must recognize that the future threat to peace and stability is increasingly Poverty, not Communism."

"If all Communists on earth disappeared overnight," former ambassador to India Chester Bowles pointed out, "the need for helping struggling peoples to achieve a democratic society would still be here."

All parts of our earth have been drawn closer together, and made interdependent, by modern communications, satellites, supersonic flights, and multinational corporations.

"This makes essential a global, as opposed to regional, approach to food, energy, capital, and development," wrote Bill Moyers in *Newsweek,* "and it makes what happens especially in the truly destitute nations impossible to ignore."

Borlaug pointed out, "There can be no real and lasting comfort in any corner of the world when one talks about food. We dream of isolation—of being free of the effects and outcome of the spreading problem of hunger. Yet our isolation will be shattered by poverty and misery in immense areas of the earth."

But doesn't charity, in any event, begin at home? Many Americans feel that the race against time is not really *their* race. Why worry about those in need abroad, when we have such a long way to go to care properly for needy Americans?

"This question is unanswerable," observed Desmond

King-Hele, deputy chief scientific officer of the Royal Aircraft Establishment, "as long as nationalism remains strong. Only if we recognize that we all belong to one world village now—that we know as much about remote trouble-spots as about the next street—shall we admit the claims of the needy from all countries."

The global view holds that an accident of birth, the geography of where you happen to be born, should not determine whether you get enough to eat. What crime did children in the Sahel and Bangladesh commit to be doomed to die of starvation by the millions?

There are also practical reasons for helping the hungry nations. American prosperity depends upon world trade— selling our surplus production overseas, importing the raw materials we need. The more we assist poorer nations, the more of our products they can buy, and the more we may continue to have access to their raw materials at a fair price.

Hunger anywhere in the world is also a threat to peace, especially when a government runs out of farmland for its starving people. In July 1969 hundreds of thousands of hungry farmers in El Salvador, the most densely populated country in Central America, poured across the border into Honduras and began farming vacant land. Honduran troops sought to drive them out in a five-day war which was ended by a truce arranged by the Organization of American States. But clashes over the disputed land continue.

Some writers sympathize with the right of a hungry nation to seize a portion of territory not needed or used by another country. But acting on this assumption overcrowded nations of Asia would be entitled to invade sprawling, lightly populated land masses like Siberia, Australia, and Canada.

Another possible danger is the struggle between powers for the right to control the weather in order to bring rain to drought-stricken farmlands. At a UN conference on overpopulation held in Bucharest, Romania, in August 1974,

" . . . we all belong to one world village now." (WIDE WORLD PHOTOS, *left*; FAO, *right*)

Lester Brown predicted that overpopulation and food short-ages may eventually provoke nations into rivalry for control of seedable coulds; perhaps even to the extent of all-out meteorological warfare.

U.S. general William H. Draper warned complacent Amer-icans, "The population explosion can shatter *your* world."

War and dictatorship are distinct possibilities when drought and crop failure are followed by unrelieved hunger. Desperate people respond to demagogues, and demagogues tend to become dictators whose only solution is military conquest. Seneca warned in the time of the Caesars, "A hungry people listens not to reason, nor cares for justice, nor is bent by prayer." Julius Caesar himself is reputed to have said, "It's not these well-fed men I fear, but the pale and hungry's face."

Above all, there is the question of whether the American conscience will permit us to let millions of people perish of hunger without lifting a hand to save them. As C. P. Snow predicted, we may soon be watching one-third of the world starve to death on our color TV sets. If our reaction is simply to flick the dial to a comedy program or football game, we will be fiddling while Rome burns—paving the way for world conflict between the haves and have-nots.

Snow went on to warn: "To make the world safe while there is time, the rich countries would have to devote up to 20 per cent of their GNP [gross national product] for a period of ten to fifteen years. Obviously that would mean a radical decrease in military expenditure; it would mean that the standard of living would stay still, and then decrease."

Americans need to recognize that they, too, could suddenly find themselves in a panicky race against mass starvation if, with no reserves to fall back upon, changing weather patterns brought terrible drought and floods to North America.

Growing concern at the possibility that dangerous food shortages might happen here was evident in the early 1970's when the *New York Times* declared, "Signs point to a devastating food shortage." The *National Observer* ran the headline: FOOD EXPERTS FEAR SHORT U.S. SUPPLIES, GLOBAL STARVATION, AS SURPLUSES DWINDLE, PRICES SOAR. It went on to say, "This time the doomsayers aren't talking just about squalor in India, but also shortages, high prices, and maybe even rationing in the United States." A headline in the *Los Angeles Times* read: LOS ANGELES POLICE TRAIN FOR FOOD RIOTS.

If all food production were to stop today, no fresh milk would be available tomorrow. Eggs and red meat would be gone in five days, chicken in seven, and within a month all dried and condensed milk would have been sold. Supermarkets have only a three-to-five-day food supply, which could be wiped out within hours.

Prudence would suggest we pressure Congress to pass legislation providing food reserves against just such calamities.

In 1973 and 1974 the United States provided approximately a third of the international relief effort. But during 1974–75 many hungry nations found themselves deprived of this amount of gift aid from America's dwindling grain reserves. Dr. John Knowles, head of the Rockefeller Foundation, noted that the world food market had become governed by "price rationing." Those countries with the money got needed grain; others went hungry. In the opinion of UN experts, thirty-two were so short of food and so poor that they were threatened with mass starvation and bankruptcy.

"It's becoming increasingly obvious that this situation can't go on," admitted one Chicago grain dealer. Theodore Hesburgh, president of Notre Dame, suggested that the president set up an American "food czar" of cabinet rank to mastermind U.S. policy in providing food to needy nations.

At the World Food Conference, the United States insisted that the world should begin looking to the newly rich Arab nations, which were raking in huge oil profits, to help foot the costs of feeding the world's hungry. In actual fact, the Arabs, according to Norman Michie of the FAO, have been generous in helping some of the underdeveloped nations, but in keeping with Islamic teachings have sought to keep their contributions private.

Third World anger at the United States for its reluctance to help more erupted at a June 1975 session of the World Food Council, which emerged out of the Conference as its action arm. More than ninety of the have-not nations demanded the resignation of its American chairman. One Third World delegate asked angrily whether, if a child were drowning and others refused to save it, the powerful United States would also be justified in turning its back.

Ironically, the American news media are more apt to sentimentalize the plight of a drowning child. When a small boy in upper New York State fell down an abandoned well, details of his rescue were flashed to a deeply moved and worried public hour after hour by radio and national wire services, until the media happily reported his rescue. That same night millions of American children went to bed hungry, unnoticed and ignored.

To some extent American reluctance to do more for the world's hungry reflects a lack of awareness of their plight. What is not constantly visible is easily forgotten.

"Emergencies dramatize matters," declared UNICEF official John Balcomb. "Streams of journalists and VIP's visited the refugee camps near Calcutta. People in Europe and America saw children near the point of death on television news clips and the public response all over the world was generous. Unfortunately, none of these visitors stayed long enough to investigate the 100 million or so young children growing up under normal conditions of deprivation in India. . . . He would have found no dearth of sights to move him to compassion and alarm." But permanent emergencies do not make news.

In a recent year, when millions suffered from lack of food at home and abroad, the *Yearbook of American Churches* noted that the nation's church bodies spent more than one billion dollars for new church construction.

One is tempted to think of the magnificent temples of Egypt, built at a time when, we read in the Book of Job, those "barren with want and hunger, who gnawed in the wilderness, disfigured with calamity and misery . . . ate grass, and bark of trees, and the root of junipers was their food."

In the race against time to prevent hunger from decimating the earth, individual contributions count. If each of us helps in any way he or she can, that could represent more than 200 million combined efforts in the United States alone . . . a powerful force to set in action.

Testifying before the Foreign Relations Committee, Mother Teresa, the noted nun working in the slums of Calcutta, pleaded with Americans, "In the name of the poor of the whole world, don't miss the *chance* of giving until it hurts."

Certainly it would cost us little to stop the waste of valuable resources for nonessential purposes. James Grant, president of the Overseas Development Council, observed in 1974 that if Americans would forgo and donate the extra fertilizer they spread on their lawns, golf courses, and cemeteries, it would be more than enough to make up for the shortages which are causing crop failures abroad.

One small sacrifice we could make would be to keep fewer pets per family. Those we have now consume enough meat each year to feed 35 million of the world's hungry.

We could also increase our food supply considerably if

enough of us indulged ourselves in fewer (preferably no) cigarettes and less liquor and red meat. Many fields now raising tobacco, cattle grain, and grain for alcohol could be turned over to producing more grain for human consumption.

We might also try to be better meal planners, less wasteful with the food we buy, and contribute the savings to the hungry overseas. A study of thrown-out food in Tucson, made by a University of Arizona team headed by Professor William J. Rathje, found that American families consign more than 9 per cent of their food dollar to the garbage can. Tucson residents were shown to throw out $11 million worth of edible food annually, part as leftovers, part as spoilage because kept too long.

"I have just returned from inspecting CARE operations in the African countries of Niger, Chad, Nigeria and Kenya." reported Executive Director Frank L. Goffio in the spring of 1975. "The appalling loss of life that followed last year's crippling drought has lessened somewhat, yet long lines of hungry people still depend upon our food." He added that in India "in vast rural areas, suffering and death show no sign of lessening."

CARE estimates that $5 can provide nutritious food for 270 children, $10 can provide poor farmers with two days of training in techniques of growing more food, and $50 can equip a family with the necessary tools, seeds, fertilizer, and other essential equipment to help them feed themselves.

Personal contributions, as well as volunteered services, can be offered to organizations actively rendering food aid around the world.

These include Africare, American Freedom from Hunger Foundation, American Friends Service Committee (Quakers), American Jewish Joint Distribution Committee, American National Red Cross, CARE, Catholic Relief Services,

Church World Services, Lutheran World Relief, Oxfam-America, United States Committee for UNICEF, World Relief Commission, Inc., World University Service, and World Vision International.

One Cornell University student, given a $1,000 check as a graduation gift by his parents, decided to invest it in humanity. He signed it over to UNICEF for famine relief. Other Cornell students organized a Coalition for the Right to Eat, skipping $4,000 worth of meals and donating their cost.

In a suburb of Eugene, Oregon, forty high school students went on a "Hunger-a-thon" for thirty hours, donating $400 collected from sponsors who paid each one 25¢ per hour fasted. Junior high students in the Hispanic neighborhood of Williamsburg, Brooklyn, went without lunchtime candy and ice cream to raise a relief fund for hungry children overseas.

Some Americans believe that the primary obligation for food relief should rest on the government, rather than on the generosity of individuals and private groups. But others resent giving foreign aid because the United States, which has done so much to feed the hungry overseas, is often criticized for not doing all that it could, rather than receiving thanks for its efforts.

Still others feel that instead of simply supplying "handouts," the well-to-do governments should be providing a long-range program to give hungry nations the wherewithal they need to produce enough food to feed their own people. "If we had given them that equipment," pointed out Lord Ritchie Calder, "they would have had the food they desperately needed that much quicker."

The FAO has drawn up a World Plan for Agricultural Development, based on the needs and priorities of countries and regions up to the year 2000. Whether it is ever implemented depends in a large measure on American support.

Orville Freeman said: "Instead of trying to feed the world, we must work at top speed and with tireless determination toward the only possible long-term answer: the bulk of the world's food must be produced where it is consumed. Countries with capital and know-how and countries with hungry people must form a partnership to mobilize the resources needed to increase total food production, whether through cultivating new lands or through increasing yields on existing farmlands."

The overcrowding on earth also makes it essential that every acre of land on earth become more fully productive. The FAO reported, "The loss of cultivated land caused by erosion, urbanization, pollution, and other depredations is increasing at an alarming rate. . . . The problem of land and that of water . . . assumes still greater seriousness when projected into the future." More land must be put under cultivation using scientific technology to make it fertile.

The International Federation of Institutes for Advanced Study in Bonn has warned that all nations must lose no time in preparing for climate changes on earth that could cause major crop failures and mass starvation. It urges an immediate collective effort to build up world food reserves, with a system to channel aid swiftly to nations struck by catastrophe. An early-warning system is essential to spotlight impending famine anywhere on earth in time to prevent it.

Developing nations must not permit national pride to stand in the way of reporting famine conditions early enough. In Ethiopia, although rainfall and harvests had been declining dangerously for eight consecutive years, the government failed to signal the need for help until April 1973. It was October before international emergency aid could reach Ethiopia in effective amounts, by which time hundreds of thousands of Ethiopians were already dying.

The race against time must also include broad-scale efforts to extend the Green Revolution, not just by developing bigger and better "miracle" grains that will thrive in the hungry nations, but also by developing every possible new source of protein and vitamins not presently being utilized.

The race against time also needs more idealistic young

Americans willing to go overseas to help the world's hungry nations become self-sufficient. Orville Freeman suggested that the government finance two years of training for Peace Corps volunteers at agricultural colleges in return for two years of service in one of the underdeveloped countries. In his opinion, "Trained young people, who bring enthusiasm, energy, and the simple willingness to dirty their hands in the world's fields and farm sheds can make a decisive contribution to increasing food production."

The World Food Conference called for a concerted effort by the world's wealthy nations to produce more food, and give more money and technical assistance, to combat hunger around the globe. But food experts point out that it is also essential for the hungry nations to do more to help themselves.

They must raise fewer cash crops, and more crops to feed their own people. They must move toward land reform. They must revitalize and irrigate their soil to increase crop yields. They must crack down on officials who profiteer on food aid. They must build more roads for food distribution.

Above all, they must reduce or halt the increase in their population by family-planning programs. The rich nations must also join them in seeking zero population growth. As C. P. Snow insisted, there must be "no more people than the earth can take."

Hunger on planet earth is a grave problem, but it is not an insurmountable problem. Believers in American know-how think that this country could make the difference, if there were an aroused national determination to wipe out hunger once and for all, both at home and abroad. Evidence is growing that average Americans are beginning to be concerned with the right of everyone to food.

At a televised town meeting in Jacksonville, Florida, racing driver Peter Gregg declared: "Compared to building a supersonic airliner or landing men on the moon, the technology is simple, the solution is simple, and the means are in this country to solve the hunger problem. . . . Let's not blame Congress, let's not blame anybody—let's blame ourselves. We haven't wanted to spend the money to feed the hungry. And that, gentlemen, is the fact."

Our race against hunger is far more momentous than the race to the moon to which President John Kennedy challenged the Russians. Few Americans then objected that the space program would cost us ten times more than we spend a year in food aid. It took ten years, 20,000 contractors, 300,000 technicians, and $24 billion to put a man on the moon.

Suppose we put that same awesome amount of time, money, talent, and effort into a crash program to erase hunger from our own planet. Which, today, would mean more to mankind?

If the Russians and Americans combined forces on earth, as they are now doing in space, few can doubt that these two superpowers alone would be able to turn aside the famine that threatens those on earth by the year 2000. Throwing all their vast scientific resources into the struggle, they could irrigate the Sahara, turning it into a lush farming region whose crops could feed the whole African continent.

They could build fertilizer plants operated by solar energy all over the globe, making the soil productive for small farmers everywhere. They could provide agricultural kits and services for every hungry nation to enable its people to feed themselves. They could organize family-planning programs that would halt the world's reckless population explosion.

Whether the United States moves in these directions will depend greatly on the instructions tomorrow's young voters give their representatives in Congress.

Which way will our rising generation take us—toward disaster on planet earth, or toward peace and plenty for all?

Bibliography and Suggested Further Reading

(*Indicates recommended reading)

Adler, Ruth, ed. *The Working Press.* New York: Bantam Books, 1970.

Aldrich, Daniel G., Jr. *Research for the World Food Crisis.* Washington, D.C.: American Association for the Advancement of Science, 1970.

Archer, Jules. *RIOT! A History of Mob Action in the United States.* New York: Hawthorn Books, 1974.

———. *The Russians and the Americans.* New York: Hawthorn Books, 1975.

Arévalo, Juan José. *Anti-Kommunism in Latin America.* New York: Lyle Stuart, 1963.

*Bagdikian, Ben H. *In the Midst of Plenty.* New York: New American Library, 1964.

Baron, Stanley. *The Desert Locust.* New York: Charles Scribner's Sons, 1972.

*Bickel, Lennard. *Facing Starvation.* New York: Reader's Digest Press, 1974.

*Borgstrom, George. *Hungry Planet.* New York: Macmillan, 1967.

*———. *Too Many.* New York: Macmillan, 1967.

Bowles, Chester. *Promises to Keep.* New York: Harper & Row, 1971.

Bridger, Gordon. *Famine in Retreat, the Fight vs. Hunger.* New York: International Publications Service, 1970.

*Brown, Lester R. *Seeds of Change.* New York: Praeger, 1970.

Burnell, Elaine H., and von Simson, Piers, eds. *Pacem in Maribus: Ocean Enterprises.* Santa Barbara: Center for the Study of Democratic Institutions, 1970.

*Citizens' Board of Inquiry. *Hunger, U.S.A.* Boston: Beacon Press, 1969.

*Clark, Colin. *Starvation or Plenty?* New York: Taplinger, 1970.

Committee of Concerned Asian Scholars. *China! Inside the People's Republic.* New York: Bantam Books, 1972.

Commoner, Barry. *Science and Survival.* New York: Viking Press, 1966.

*De Bell, Garrett, ed. *The Environmental Handbook.* New York: Ballantine Books, 1970.

Doubleday, Thomas. *True Law of Population.* New York: Kelley, 1847.

Dubos, René; Pines, Maya; and the Editors of LIFE. *Health and Disease.* New York: Time, 1965.

Duvignaud, Jean. *Change at Shebika: Report from a North African Village.* New York: Pantheon Books, 1970.

*Ehrlich, Paul R. *The Population Bomb.* New York: Ballantine Books, 1971.

*Freeman, Orville L. *World Without Hunger.* New York: Praeger, 1968.

Gunther, John. *Inside South America.* New York: Harper & Row, 1967.

Halacy, D. S. *The Geometry of Hunger.* New York: Harper's Magazine Press, 1972.

*Hamsun, Knut. *Hunger.* New York: Farrar, Straus & Giroux, 1967.

Holden, Frances. *Study of the Effect of Starvation.* Baltimore: Williams & Wilkins, 1926.

*Hollings, Ernest F. *The Case Against Hunger.* New York: Cowles, 1970.

Johnson, Lyndon Baines. *The Vantage Point.* New York: Popular Library, 1971.

Kahin, George McTurnan, and Lewis, John W. *The United States in Vietnam.* New York: Dial Press, 1967.

Kervin, Peter. *Poverty and Wealth.* Valley Forge, Pa.: Judson Press, 1971.

King-Hele, Desmond. *The End of the Twentieth Century?* New York: St. Martin's Press, 1970.

*Kotz, Nick. *Let Them Eat Promises.* Garden City, N.Y.: Doubleday, 1971.

*Lens, Sidney. *Poverty Yesterday and Today.* New York: Thomas Y. Crowell, 1973.

Leuchtenburg, William E. *Franklin D. Roosevelt and the New Deal.* New York: Harper & Row, 1963.

Lindqvist, Sven. *China in Crisis.* New York: Thomas Y. Crowell, 1963.

MacLaine, Shirley. *You Can Get There from Here.* New York: W. W. Norton, 1975.

Martin, John Bartlow. *Overtaken by Events.* Garden City, N.Y.: Doubleday, 1966.

May, Jacques M., and McClellan, Donna L. *The Ecology of Malnutrition in Eastern Africa and Four Countries of Western Africa.* New York: Hafner, 1970.

*Milbauer, Barbara, and Leinwand, Gerald. *Hunger.* New York: Pocket Books, 1971.

*Miller, Miriam, ed. *The Neglected Years: Early Childhood.* New York: United Nations Children's Fund, 1973.

*Moomaw, I. W. *The Challenge of Hunger.* New York: Praeger, 1967.

*Nair, Kusum. *The Lonely Furrow: Farming in the United States, Japan, and India.* Ann Arbor: University of Michigan Press, 1969.

Nehemkis, Peter. *Latin America: Myth and Reality.* New York: New American Library, 1966.

*Ogg, Elizabeth. *Population and the American Future.* New York: Public Affairs Committee, 1974.

Orwell, George. *Down and Out in Paris and London.* New York: Avon, 1933.

Paddock, William and Paul. *Famine—1975.* Boston: Little, Brown, 1967.

Pearson, Frank A., and Harper, Floyd A. *The World's Hunger.* Ithaca, N.Y.: Cornell University Press, 1945.

*Pilisuk, Marc and Phyllis. *Poor Americans: How the White Poor Live.* Chicago: Aldine, 1971.

Pirie, N. W. *Food Resources.* Baltimore: Penguin Books, 1969.

Radosh, Ronald. *American Labor and United States Foreign Policy.* New York: Random House, 1969.

Reckord, Barry. *Does Fidel Eat More Than Your Father?* New York: Praeger, 1971.

Reed, John. *Insurgent Mexico.* New York: International, 1970.

*Rienow, Robert, and Train, Leona. *Moment in the Sun.* New York: Ballantine Books, 1967.

*Sax, Karl. *Standing Room Only: The World's Exploding Population.* Boston: Beacon Press, 1969.

Schurmann, Franz, and Schell, Orville, eds. *Communist China: 1949 to the Present.* New York: Random House, 1967.

Segal, Judith A. *Food for the Hungry: the Reluctant Society.* Baltimore: Johns Hopkins Press, 1970.

Segal, Ronald. *The Race War.* New York: Bantam Books, 1967.

*Snow, C. P. *State of Siege.* New York: Charles Scribner's Sons, 1969.

Snow, Edgar. *The Long Revolution.* New York: Random House, 1972.

———. *Red Star over China.* New York: Grove Press, 1961.

Stakman, E. *Campaign Against Hunger.* Cambridge, Mass.: Harvard University Press, 1967.

*Stewart, George R. *Ordeal By Hunger.* New York: Pocket Books, 1974.

*Stewart, Maxwell S. *Hunger in America.* New York: Public Affairs Committee, 1970.

*———. *Food for the World's Hungry.* New York: Public Affairs Committee, 1974.

Subcommittee on Department Operations of the House Committee of Agriculture. *World Population and Food Supply and Demand Situation.* Washington, D.C.: U.S. Government Printing Office, 1974.

Sweet, J. Stouder. *Poverty in the U.S.A.* New York: Public Affairs Committee, 1967.

Terkel, Studs. *Working.* New York: Avon, 1974.

*Walford, Cornelius. *The Famines of the World: Past and Present.* London: Edward Stanford, 1879.

*Wilson, Charles Morrow. *The Fight Against Hunger.* New York: Funk & Wagnalls, 1969.

Also consulted were publications of American Friends Service Committee, Community Churches of America, Center for Disease Control, the Cousteau Society, Environmental Defense Fund, Food and Agriculture Organization of the United Nations, the Planned Parenthood Federation, Quaker United Nations Office, Rural Advancement Fund, UNICEF, and the U.S. Department of Agriculture.

Also issues of *America, Boston Globe, Center Magazine, Center Reports, Ceres, Christian Century, Christianity Today, Commonweal, Ebony, Esquire, Harper's Magazine, Lithopinion, Moneysworth, Ms., The Nation, Newsweek, New Republic, The New York Times, The New York Times Magazine, The New York Post, Philadelphia Inquirer, Reader's Digest, Saturday Review/World, Science, Science News, Time, TV Guide, UNICEF News, U.S. News and World Report, Variety,* and *World Health.*

Index